CENTRE FOR CO-OPERATION WITH THE

Labour Market
Policies
in
Slovenia

ORGANISATION FOR ECONOMIC CO-OPERATION AND DEVELOPMENT

ORGANISATION FOR ECONOMIC CO-OPERATION AND DEVELOPMENT

Pursuant to Article 1 of the Convention signed in Paris on 14th December 1960, and which came into force on 30th September 1961, the Organisation for Economic Co-operation and Development (OECD) shall promote policies designed:

- to achieve the highest sustainable economic growth and employment and a rising standard of living in Member countries, while maintaining financial stability, and thus to contribute to the development of the world economy;
- to contribute to sound economic expansion in Member as well as non-member countries in the process of economic development; and
- to contribute to the expansion of world trade on a multilateral, non-discriminatory basis in accordance with international obligations.

The original Member countries of the OECD are Austria, Belgium, Canada, Denmark, France, Germany, Greece, Iceland, Ireland, Italy, Luxembourg, the Netherlands, Norway, Portugal, Spain, Sweden, Switzerland, Turkey, the United Kingdom and the United States. The following countries became Members subsequently through accession at the dates indicated hereafter: Japan (28th April 1964), Finland (28th January 1969), Australia (7th June 1971), New Zealand (29th May 1973), Mexico (18th May 1994), the Czech Republic (21st December 1995), Hungary (7th May 1996), Poland (22nd November 1996) and the Republic of Korea (12th December 1996). The Commission of the European Communities takes part in the work of the OECD (Article 13 of the OECD Convention).

THE CENTRE FOR CO-OPERATION WITH THE ECONOMIES IN TRANSITION

The Centre for Co-operation with the European Economies in Transition (CCEET), which serves as the focal point for co-operation between the OECD and the countries of Central and Eastern Europe, was created in March 1990. In 1991, the activities of the Centre were expanded to include the New Independent States of the former Soviet Union, and subsequently Mongolia (1992) and Vietnam (1995). In 1993, to take account of its broader geographical focus, the Centre was renamed the Centre for Co-operation with the Economies in Transition (CCET).

The Centre operates a number of Special Country Programmes: the Partners in Transition (PIT) Programme, of which the last remaining "Partner", the Slovak Republic is negotiating accession to the OECD (the other former "Partners" – the Czech Republic, Hungary and Poland – have joined the OECD); the Russian Federation Programme; and the country-specific programmes for Bulgaria, Romania and Slovenia.

Publié en français sous le titre :
POLITIQUES DU MARCHÉ DU TRAVAIL EN SLOVÉNIE

FOREWORD

Previously one of the most advanced centrally planned economies, Slovenia's transition to a market economy has proceeded relatively smoothly compared with most other Central and Eastern European countries. Employment levels declined in the initial years of the transition, but the situation improved subsequently. The reduction in employment was concentrated among individuals under age 25 and over 50 years of age, which reflected a higher rate of participation in post-secondary education and increased earlier retirement. Employment rates among prime working-age individuals, in contrast, remained high compared with other transition countries.

The relatively smooth transition process is attributable in part to the cautious approach to enterprise restructuring. This report argues that conditions are now favourable for implementing a faster pace of restructuring in order to further reduce the numbers of inefficient firms. The report also proposes that consideration should be given to reducing certain burdensome administrative functions of the National Employment Office, thereby enabling it to focus its resources more on core functions, such as job placement and counselling of the unemployed. Ways of promoting higher labour force participation rates among youth and older age groups also are suggested.

This review was conducted as part of the programme of the OECD's Centre for Co-operation with the Economies in Transition (CCET) and was discussed by the OECD's Employment, Labour and Social Affairs Committee in Ljubljana in February 1997.

This volume is published on the responsibility of the Secretary-General of the OECD.

TABLE OF CONTENTS

Chapter 4

Social policies affecting the labour market

Tables

Charts

INTRODUCTION: THE COUNTRY,
ITS PEOPLE AND HISTORY

With two million inhabitants, Slovenia is one of the smallest nation-states in Europe, comparable in size to the former Yugoslav Republic of Macedonia or the Baltic states of Estonia and Latvia. The people are predominantly Roman Catholic and speak Slovene, a South Slavic language distinct from other tongues in the group, such as Serbo-Croat.

Slovenia lies in the most south-easterly region of the Alps and at the northern end of the Adriatic Sea, where the coastal district has at times been dominated by Venetian merchants. To the east, Slovenia faces the Pannonian plain, part of the vast lowland area that stretches across Hungary, northern Croatia, Vojvodina and other regions, all of which were ruled by Hungary before 1918.

In contrast to neighbouring Croatia, Slovenia's ties have been with Austria rather than with Hungary since the Middle Ages, apart from periods of Turkish invasion and intervention by France under Napoleon. The attachment to Austria was confirmed at the Congress of Vienna in 1815, and again in 1867, when the Hapsburg empire was reorganised in two parts as a "double monarchy". In effect, Slovenia shares much of its history not only with what is now Austria, but also with Lombardy, Veneto, Friuli, the Czech lands and southern Poland. Its aristocracy and cities were largely German-speaking until this century, but culture has flourished in the Slovene language for a relatively long time, for instance during the Enlightenment.

At the end of World War I, Slovenia was a founding member nation of the first State of Slovenes, Croats and Serbs, later known as Yugoslavia. This State, however, was soon reshaped against the will of the Slovenes into a kingdom with a centralised and authoritarian style of government. After World War II, when Slovenia had been divided between different occupying powers, it was one of six republics in the Socialist Federal Republic of Yugoslavia until it declared itself independent by referendum in 1990. Its sovereignty was *de facto* unchallenged after the failure of a brief federal army attack in mid-1991, and it gained international recognition by the end of that year.

THE TRANSITION AND ITS LABOUR MARKET IMPLICATIONS

THE GENERAL ECONOMY

Slovenia was the richest republic in Yugoslavia, and it was also more economically advanced than other transition countries in Central and Eastern Europe. It has maintained a relative advantage after the transition, with for example a GDP per capita which in terms of purchasing power parities (PPPs) is slightly higher than in the Czech Republic, the second-richest transition country, although still about 15 per cent lower than in Greece, the least wealthy member of the European Union. Slovenia's lead over other transition countries appears as substantially greater if GDP is measured by current exchange rates, because its currency, the Tolar – as the first transition currency – has attained a foreign-exchange value almost as high as its domestic purchasing power[1]. The levels of employment and labour force participation are also relatively high. Unemployment, as measured by labour force surveys, peaked at 9 per cent in 1993 and 1994 and has since fallen to about 7.5 per cent, *i.e.* near the OECD average and lower than the averages for both Eastern and Western Europe.

The economy contracted in the early 1990s, as in all transition countries, but the output shock was comparatively moderate, with an accumulated real GDP decline of less than one-fifth between 1989 and 1992 (Chart 1.1). In this respect, developments in Slovenia were similar to those in the Czech Republic, Hungary and Poland, but substantially less disruptive than in most other transition countries. GDP growth resumed in the second half of 1993, *i.e.* earlier than in most comparable countries except Poland, and real GDP is now close to the pre-transition level[2]. Real wages initially fell more than GDP, especially during Yugoslavia's hyperinflation in 1990; they have been growing since February 1992, but remain below an inflationary peak value briefly attained in 1989.

The economic growth from 1993 to 1995 was driven to a considerable extent by investments, which increased their share in GDP from 20 to 23 per cent, with a further investment growth in 1996. This is due in part to large investments in roads and telecommunications, and also to business investment. The share of the manufacturing sector in total investment was only about one-fifth in 1995, with a large

◆　Chart I.I.　**Economic developments in Central and Eastern European countries**

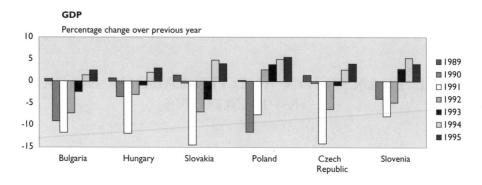

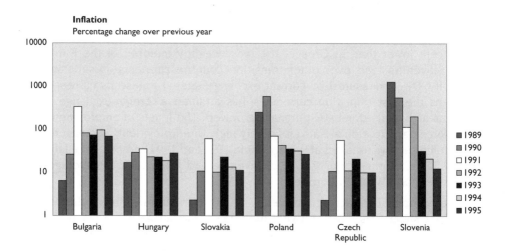

Source: OECD.

and increasing proportion in machinery rather than construction, suggesting that enterprises may have emphasised productivity enhancement more than expansion (IMAD, 1995, p. 9).

The macroeconomic stabilisation policy pursued since independence has been largely successful, bringing the inflation rate below 25 per cent from 1993 and below 10 per cent from mid-1995. The markets for capital and foreign exchange have been partly liberalised, and most institutional barriers to trade have been removed.

In the present situation, some of the key policy challenges concern the country's inevitable integration in the international economy. Many Slovenian enterprises have a long-standing orientation towards trade with the outside world, although until 1990 they were primarily occupying a prominent position in the former Yugoslav market. The country is currently highly dependent on foreign trade, with export revenues corresponding to over half of GDP – a higher export share than in most transition countries except Slovakia. Most of the trade is with the European Union, and both exports and imports are dominated by machinery and other manufactured products (Tables 1.1 and 1.2). As a result, Slovenia is sensitive to fluctuations in the conditions for trade, especially with Western Europe. This sensitivity was illustrated by a sudden decline of exports and industrial output at the beginning of 1996, apparently caused by the combination of a highly valued Tolar and economic stagnation in its main export markets.

Table 1.1. **Main trade partners**

Percentage distribution of Slovenia's exports and imports by country

	Exports				Imports			
	1992	1993	1994	1995	1992	1993	1994	1995
Germany	27	30	30	30	23	25	24	23
Italy	13	12	14	15	14	16	17	17
France	9	9	9	8	8	8	8	8
Austria	5	5	5	6	8	9	10	10
Croatia	14	12	11	11	14	9	7	6
Former Yug. Republic of Macedonia	2	3	3	2	1	1	1	0
Total	71	71	72	72	68	68	68	65

Source: *Statistical Yearbooks.*

Table 1.2. **Trade by commodity**

Percentage distribution of Slovenia's exports and imports by type of commodity

	Exports				Imports			
	1992	1993	1994	1995	1992	1993	1994	1995
Machinery, transport equipment	29	27	30	32	26	30	32	34
Products classified by material (*e.g.* rubber, wood and metal products)	27	26	27	29	20	18	19	20
Finished products (*e.g.* clothing and furniture)	23	26	24	22	11	12	11	11
Chemicals	9	9	10	10	12	12	12	12
Total	89	88	92	93	69	72	74	76

Note: The four product categories correspond to SITC 7, 6, 8 and 5, respectively.
Source: *Slovenian Monthly Economic Monitor*, 15 july, 1996.

Compared with the determined policy of macroeconomic stabilisation, the government's approach to microeconomic reform has been cautious. During several years, private-sector growth was due less to privatisation than to the creation of new small firms. Privatisation of large enterprises is now well under way, but it has suffered many delays, and, even where it has been successful, the restructuring of production has often continued to face obstacles. Institutional factors, partly a legacy of the previous Yugoslav system, seem to soften the budgetary constraints faced by enterprise managers, and so reduce the sense of urgency attached to restructuring. For example, outside shareholder interests have been muted by an element of "insider" power, which on average is likely to have exerted a conservative influence; restructuring may also have been discouraged by redundancy regulations and the fact that the government pays subsidies to preserve jobs.

The size of unresolved structural problems in enterprises is difficult to estimate, but one indication is provided by the fact that 29 per cent of the country's 31 000 commercial firms reported net losses in 1995[3]. The loss-making firms employed 170 000 persons (about one-fourth of the dependent employment in the country), and their losses were so large that the aggregate profitability of Slovenia's commercial sector appears to have been negative[4]. Major loss-making branches of activity included paper production, machine-building, metal-processing and timber production.

INSTITUTIONS INHERITED FROM THE FORMER YUGOSLAVIA

Slovenia's reform path has been broadly comparable to that of other transition countries. Like them, the country has sought to address a long-standing efficiency problem in the economy, marked by a widespread failure by enterprises to adjust their output to meet changing demands. During the 1980s, moreover, the whole of Yugoslavia had been struck by a deep economic and political crisis. The need for fundamental economic reconstruction was recognised by the federal government in 1989, i.e. at about the same time as in other parts of Central and Eastern Europe.

However, the detail of many microeconomic policy issues at stake today are related to specific institutions inherited from Yugoslavia. These included a ubiquitous set of administrative and policy-making procedures, largely designed to promote social consensus, reflecting Yugoslavia's peculiar combination of decentralisation and political control at local level. In that system, "self-management" bodies with similar status took decisions not only in enterprises, but also in public institutions such as municipalities, schools, social insurance and employment offices. Enterprises and public authorities were also interconnected by a host of administrative reporting requirements, consultations and planning, concerning for example the numbers of workers and trainees to be hired each year. A fundamental weakness of the system was that it encouraged irresponsible decisions in enterprises, as managers tried to accommodate political demands along with those of their workers. In effect, the system therefore relied on costly fund transfers to many enterprises in the form of direct subsidies, tax breaks and cheap credits.

Slovenia has now abolished "self-management" and its legal corollary, "social ownership", and the market economy is well established. Enterprises are being privatised and restructured, albeit not without problems. However, a number of administrative practices in government agencies are still in force or are being reformed only slowly. In such matters, continuity is often regarded as appropriate; indeed, some of the principles underlying the Yugoslav model, including a relatively open exchange of information between enterprises and public authorities, may even prove useful in the future, if their application can be adapted to match the requirements of a competitive market economy. In their present form, however, several of the policies that have been retained are anachronistic. Some may be merely bureaucratic, such as the obligation for employers to notify job vacancies for which they already have candidates (see Chapter 3), but others could be more problematic. The rules about measures for redundant workers, for example, could encourage preservation of an inappropriate division of responsibilities between enterprises and public authorities (Chapter 2). As a general rule, it is crucial for efficiency that enterprise managers should be able to focus on the problems of their business, within constraints set by law rather than by case-by-case decisions.

THE LABOUR MARKET

Population and labour force

Slovenia's population has been stagnant since the early 1990s, at just under 2 million, of which in 1996 some 70 per cent or 1.4 million were in the potential working-age range of 15 to 64 years. As in most European countries, the birth rate is below the level that would imply a full renewal of generations, while the share of persons aged 65 or more is 13 per cent and rising. Almost 90 per cent of the inhabitants regard themselves as Slovene by nationality, as this was defined in the former Yugoslavia. Other groups, also often citizens of Slovenia, are mainly Croats, Serbs and Slavic Muslims; there are also several smaller categories including two with a special constitutional status (Hungarians and Italians).

Labour force participation is traditionally high for men and women, except in the age groups under 25 and over 50 (see Table 1.3). For the whole 15 to 64 age group, the May 1996 labour force survey (LFS[5]) recorded a participation rate of 72 per cent for men and 62 per cent for women. The rate for youth aged 15 to 24 has fallen by over one-third during the transition years, and was only 38 per cent in 1996 – i.e., lower than in most OECD countries, albeit higher than in Belgium and

Table 1.3. **Labour force participation and employment/population ratios**

Percentage of the population, by gender and age group

	Labour force participation		Employment	
	1994	1996	1994	1996
Both genders, age 15-64	**66.4**	**66.8**	**60.3**	**61.9**
15-24	39.5	38.0	30.7	30.9
25-49	91.7	91.8	84.8	86.4
50-64	36.5	37.5	34.4	36.1
Men, age 15-64	**71.7**	**71.5**	**64.7**	**66.2**
15-24	42.2	40.2	33.2	32.6
25-49	94.7	94.2	86.6	88.3
50-64	48.9	48.9	46.2	47.1
Women, age 15-64	**61.2**	**62.0**	**56.0**	**57.7**
15-24	36.6	35.8	28.0	29.1
25-49	88.7	89.4	82.9	84.5
50-64	25.1	27.1	23.6	26.0

Source: LFS data in NSO *Rapid Reports* (1994 and 1996).

France and similar to the corresponding rates for youth in several Mediterranean countries (OECD, 1996*d*, Table B). For adults, by contrast, the labour force participation patterns have not fundamentally changed with the transition, apart from a temporary fall in the already low average retirement age, followed by some increase after 1992 (see Chapter 4). For the "prime-age" group of 25 to 49, the participation rate in 1996 was 94 per cent for men and 89 per cent for women, and thus comparable to the highest rates recorded in the OECD area (*e.g.* in the Czech Republic and Nordic countries). In general, as shown in Table 1.4 (which uses a different definition of the working-age population), Slovenia's labour force participation is higher than in most transition countries other than the Czech Republic and Russia.

The educational attainment of the labour force is broadly comparable to the situation in most OECD and transition countries (Chart 1.2 compares selected transition countries). Since the 1960s, a majority of youths entering the labour market have had some education at the post-compulsory secondary level, mostly with vocational orientation. Nevertheless, almost one-fourth of the youths who entered the labour market in recent years had only primary education (finished or not); if youths who entered but never finished secondary education are included, the proportion without qualifications was as high as one-third.

In the labour force as a whole, 76 per cent had some education at secondary level in 1996, while 14 per cent had higher education (Table 1.5). The proportion with less than two years of secondary education fell from 31 per cent in 1994 to

Table 1.4. **Labour force participation and employment/population ratios in selected transition countries**

Percentage of the working-age population

	Labour force participation			Employment		
	1993	1994	1995	1993	1994	1995
Slovenia	**77.3**	**77.5**	**76.6**	**70.1**	**70.3**	**70.8**
Bulgaria (1993 : Q3)	75.2	73.5	71.9	59.0	58.8	60.5
Czech Republic	78.8	80.2	76.6	75.9	77.2	73.8
Hungary	70.3	67.7	65.2	61.8	60.4	58.5
Poland	70.3	70.7	69.4	60.2	60.4	60.2
Slovakia	73.9	74.6	74.9	64.5	64.5	64.9
Romania (Q1)	n.a.	72.7	73.6	n.a.	65.9	66.8
Russia (Q4)	77.6	76.9	77.8	73.2	70.7	70.4

n.a.: Not available.
Note: All data refer to the *second quarter* of the years mentioned, except as noted.
This table uses the OECD/CCET definition of the working-age population, covering women aged 15 to 54 and men aged 15 to 59.
Sources: OCDE-CCET labour market database and the NSO *Rapid Report* No. 195.

◆   Chart 1.2. *Labour force by educational attainment*
Percentage distribution

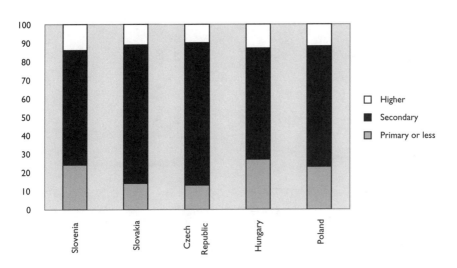

Note: The data refer to 1996 for Slovenia and 1994 for other countries.
Source: OECD-CCET labour market database.

Table 1.5. **Educational attainment**

Percentage distribution of the labour force, the employed and the unemployed

Level of education	1. Labour force		2. Employed		3. Unemployed		4. Difference between cols. 2 and 3	
	1994	1996	1994	1996	1994	1996	1994	1996
Low:								
Incomplete primary school	4.4	3.6	4.3	3.5	5.3	5.1	1.0	1.6
Primary school	21.9	20.2	21.2	19.5	29.1	28.9	7.9	9.4
One or two years in secondary school	4.5	3.0	4.2	3.0	6.8	4.0	2.6	1.0
Subtotal	**30.8**	**26.8**	**29.7**	**26.0**	**41.2**	**38.0**	**11.5**	**12.0**
Medium:								
Two or thee years in secondary school	27.0	30.4	26.8	30.2	28.5	31.9	1.7	1.7
Four or five years in secondary school	27.0	28.7	27.2	29.0	24.6	24.5	– 2.6	– 4.5
Subtotal	**54.0**	**59.1**	**54.0**	**59.2**	**53.1**	**56.4**	**– 0.9**	**– 2.8**
Higher:								
Non-university degree	7.6	7.1	8.1	7.4	2.3	3.8	– 5.8	– 3.6
University degree	6.8	6.1	7.2	6.4	3.2	1.8	– 4.0	– 4.6
Postgraduate degree	0.8	0.8	0.9	0.8	0.0	0.0	– 0.9	– 0.8
Subtotal	**15.2**	**14.0**	**16.2**	**14.6**	**5.5**	**5.6**	**– 10.7**	**– 9.0**
Total	**100**	**100**	**100**	**100**	**100**	**100**	–	–

Note: Estimates for small categories are approximate. Totals may not add up exactly to 100 due to rounding.
Source: LFS data in NSO *Rapid Reports* (1994 and 1996).

27 per cent in 1996[6]. This trend, associated with falling demand for unskilled labour (see below), was caused in part by a propensity for persons with little education to leave the labour market.

Important reforms have been begun with regard to the country's education system, notably at secondary level (see Box 1). Policy efforts have also been made to improve the provisions for adult education, which previously were neglected[7]. Currently, adult education is offered mainly in institutions for post-secondary education, which had about 10 000 part-time students in the school year 1994/95. (While regarded as adults, many of them were probably relatively young.) Only about 2 000 adults participated in secondary-school education, while probably a comparable number of training places were found in specialised institutions for adult education, *e.g.* "folk high schools", and in the private sector.

Box 1. **Reforming secondary education**

Slovenia's secondary school courses usually begin at age 15 and last for two to four years. They are intended for pupils who have completed the compulsory primary school, which will soon be extended from eight to nine years. A series of important reforms have been introduced in recent years, and the country's education system as a whole is still in a state of transition. The changes concern all kinds of education, but especially the secondary level.

From 1983 until 1988, all Yugoslav secondary schools were organised according to a model called "guided" education, which assumed in principle that all educational tracks would lead to specific occupations. Vocational elements of the instruction were organised in co-operation between schools and employers, who were also, often, expected to hire school-leavers whose education they had sponsored. At the same time, it was assumed in principle that all pupils would have a choice between leaving after two or three years or continuing through the fourth year of secondary education, which would make them eligible for higher education.

In theory, thus, the Yugoslav education system combined an egalitarian approach to academic instruction with an ambition to keep all students in contact with the labour market. However, the reality was often far from being compatible with any of these principles, which therefore were increasingly criticised as unrealistic, and often ignored.

Structure of the new system

A series of gradual changes have distanced the official policy objectives as well as the actual practice in Slovenia from the system just described. First, from

(see next page)

(*continued*)

1990, the difference in content between academic and vocational streams became more pronounced, with fewer cross-over options. Henceforth, selective four-year schools with academic orientation specialise in preparing students for university. "Technical" schools, also lasting four years, prepare students for jobs in 78 occupations, but they can also to some extent prepare them for higher education. Vocational schools offer courses for nearly 150 occupations, mostly lasting three years but sometimes only two years.

A further step, in force since 1995, was to introduce a "maturity" exam at the end of the academic secondary school, serving as an entry barrier to university. In the technical schools, pupils will from 1997 have to choose, after the second year, between a standard option that does not lead to "maturity" and a more demanding one that does.

The apparent increase in rigidity, resulting from the abolition of cross-over options, is mitigated by some special provisions for youths who have completed the three-year vocational education. They can enter a "foreman" course, which already existed, or a new type of two-year course giving them access to some forms of higher education, though not to university. If they want to enter a university, they can sometimes achieve this by following an additional six- to twelve-month course leading to "maturity". These short "maturity" courses, provided on an experimental basis, also target the graduates of non-maturity streams in technical schools.

In 1995/96, as many as 94 per cent of those leaving primary school entered some kind of secondary school, up from 88 per cent in 1990. About 22 per cent of them were enrolled in academic programmes, the others mostly going to four-year technical and three-year vocational schools. In recent years, about 12 000 students annually have entered higher education; if adults and re-entrants are excluded, the number was just under 10 000, or about one-third of the relevant youth cohorts. Most of them go to universities, but there are plans to expand the provision of non-university courses.

The role of enterprises in vocational education

While essentially school-based, vocational training in the Yugoslav system had many links with enterprises. However, after the economic transition, employers have largely withdrawn from their administrative and financial involvement in education. They have also reduced their role in paying scholarships to students, although a few firms still do so.

Nevertheless, work experience remains an important element in secondary education. It is normally organised in school workshops, but contracts with enterprises also play a role. In general, work-related activities constitute about one-third of the scheduled hours in a vocational course of secondary education. (Courses usually include 1 200 scheduled hours per year.) The remaining two-

(*see next page*)

(continued)

thirds of the time is devoted to equal parts of general education and vocational theory. In the four-year technical schools, 8 per cent of the scheduled hours are devoted to work experience.

As an alternative option, the government has begun to introduce a *"dual"* or *apprenticeship* model for vocational education, with essentially the same content as the school-based courses. This does not alter the basic content and structure of secondary education; but enterprises provide most of the instruction, apart from general education, which may therefore be concentrated in the first year. The total number of scheduled hours per week is higher in the dual system, the difference consisting of additional hours of work experience. Currently, about 10 per cent of the three-year vocational programmes follow this dual model. Some expansion is foreseen, but the system is still regarded as an experiment, to be phased in very slowly, depending on the interest shown by employers and students.

◆ Chart 1.3. **Employment according to different data sources**
Thousands of persons

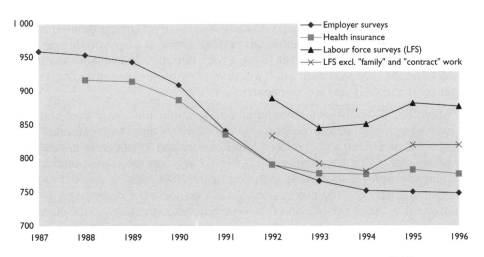

Note: The data derived from the health insurance do not include farmers, probably numbering about 55 000.
The categories "unpaid family work" and "contract and other work" are included only in the highest LFS-based curve.
Sources: See text.

Employment

Employment probably fell by between 10 and 15 per cent during the initial transition period. The exact size of the decline is not known because available data for the years prior to 1992 do not cover all types of employment (Chart 1.3 compares employment data from the principal sources). Perhaps most suitable for comparison over time are the register-based statistics about employed persons covered by health insurance, which indicate an accumulated decline of 15 per cent, occurring essentially between 1989 and 1993 (*Statistical Yearbook*, Table 10-6). This source disregards a possible increase in so-called contract work, unpaid family work and work for less than 18 hours a week. Compared with similar sources in other transition countries, it suggests that the fall in employment was relatively small in Slovenia, but greater than in the Czech Republic and about as great as in the Slovak Republic. As an alternative data source, the National Statistical Office (NSO) compiles data from employer surveys, showing an employment reduction of over 20 per cent from 1987 to 1994. This, however, is likely to reflect a more substantial element of under-reporting of several types of work[8].

Total employment fell slightly between 1995 and 1996 according to the LFS, but remained 3 per cent higher than in 1994. The figure for 1996 implies a higher employment/population ratio for working ages than in most comparable countries, again with the Czech Republic as a chief exception (Table 1.4).

The impression of a high employment level in Slovenia is even more striking if one takes into account that a large majority work full-time. Only some 15 000 of the ordinary wage and salary earners (2 per cent) had part-time jobs in May 1996, but to this figure must be added some 34 000 part-timers who were either self-employed, contract workers or unpaid family workers. (Part-time is defined as less than 36 hours per week.) Altogether, about 6 per cent of employment was part-time – a proportion similar to that in the Czech Republic and higher than in the Slovak Republic (2.3 per cent), but lower than in most other countries, *e.g.* Poland (9 per cent) and Germany (16 per cent).

About 120 000 persons in dependent employment, full-time or part-time, did not have a permanent employee status. About 60 000 of them had temporary jobs, while 20 000 had "contract" or related forms of work and 38 000 were unpaid family workers (Table 1.6). For comparison, Table 1.7 presents the corresponding data according to employer surveys, as compiled by the NSO, indicating also the size of discrepancies between the two sources. As can be seen, the discrepancy in total employment between the LFS and this NSO source was greater than the sum of all mentioned forms of employment other than a permanent employee status or self-employment.

The number of the self-employed, other than farmers, increased from about 30 000 in the late 1980s to about 54 000 in 1996. With farmers included, self-

Table 1.6. **The labour force, employment and unemployment according to labour force surveys**

	1992	1993	1994	1995	1996
Labour force	**969 000**	**931 000**	**934 000**	**952 000**	**947 000**
Employment	**889 000**	**845 000**	**851 000**	**882 000**	**877 000**
a. Employees	718 000	688 000	676 000	713 000	710 000
– permanent	n.a.	644 000	628 000	660 000	650 000
– temporary	n.a.	44 000	48 000	53 000	60 000
Of which part-time (perm. or temporary)	n.a.	15 000	13 000	15 000	15 000
b. Self-employed	115 000	103 000	104 000	108 000	109 000
c. Family workers	38 000	28 000	46 000	40 000	38 000
d. "Contract work" and related forms of work	17 000	26 000	24 000	21 000	20 000
Unemployment	**80 000**	**86 000**	**86 000**	**70 000**	**70 000**
– as percentage of the labour force	8.3	9.2	9.1	7.3	7.4
Memorandum items:					
Persons who stated they were receiving unemployment benefits (income-related or flat-rate)	n.a.	56 000	54 000	41 000	35 000
Persons who regarded themselves as unemployed but were classified as not in the labour force	n.a.	22 000	30 000	24 000	32 000

n.a.: Not available.
Sources: NSO, OECD.

employment accounted for 109 000 jobs or 12.5 per cent of total employment in 1996, a share similar to that in the Czech Republic, Hungary and Russia but much lower than in Poland and Romania.

The share of industry in LFS employment was 42 per cent in 1996, *i.e.* higher than in any OECD country except the Czech Republic, in spite of a falling trend (Table 1.8). According to the employer surveys, the industry share in total employment fell by 6 percentage points between 1990 and 1995, while the service sector increased by a similar amount, notably in education, health and personal services. By 1996, the service sector accounted for 48 per cent of LFS employment, still a low proportion by most international standards.

Labour turnover in enterprises has increased, as shown by information about separations as a percentage of non-agricultural employment. The annual separation rate was about 13 per cent before 1990, but almost 20 per cent thereafter

Table 1.7. **The labour force, employment and unemployment according to official employer surveys and unemployment registers**

	1989	1990	1991	1992	1993	1994	1995	1996
Labour force	971 700	954 000	916 400	893 600	895 500	879 400	871 700	866 700
Employment	943 500	909 400	841 300	791 000	766 400	752 300	750 200	748 300
Employees	850 400	817 100	742 700	690 300	663 800	647 100	642 500	638 800
– in firms with 3 or more employees	819 100	785 200	709 600	657 000	626 800	605 300	593 800	585 500
– in small firms	31 300	31 900	33 100	33 300	37 000	41 800	48 700	53 200
Self-employed	93 100	92 300	98 600	100 800	102 600	105 200	107 700	109 600
– farmers	56 000	55 600	55 700	55 500	55 500	55 500	55 500	55 000
– other	37 100	36 700	42 900	45 100	47 100	49 700	52 200	54 000
Registered unemployment	**28 200**	**44 600**	**75 100**	**102 600**	**129 100**	**127 100**	**121 500**	**118 300**
– as percentage of the labour force	2.9	4.7	8.2	11.5	14.4	14.4	13.9	13.7
Recipients of								
unemployment benefits	n.a	n.a	45 900	50 800	62 600	42 500	34 200	37 800
– income-related	n.a	n.a	31 800	32 500	42 600	31 500	28 300	33 700
– flat-rate	n.a	n.a	14 100	18 200	20 100	11 000	5 900	4 100
Certain groups of unemployed persons who are usually not eligible for benefits:								
– registered for over 3 years	n.a	n.a	n.a	n.a	19 700	26 000	32 100	30 000
– first-job seekers	8 200	11 800	16 700	20 700	24 500	24 100	23 900	23 200
– others with under 12 months of work	n.a	n.a	n.a	n.a	n.a	13 000	13 300	12 000
Memorandum: discrepancies compared with LFS data:								
– for the labour force	n.a.	n.a.	n.a.	– 75 400	– 35 200	– 57 100	– 79 900	– 80 000
– for unemployment	– 6 800	– 7 400	– 2 900	– 22 600	43 400	41 600	51 900	48 700
– for total employment	n.a.	n.a.	n.a.	– 98 000	– 78 600	– 98 700	– 131 800	– 128 700
– for employees (excl. family and contract work, etc.)	n.a.	n.a.	n.a.	– 27 700	– 24 200	– 28 900	– 70 500	– 71 200
– for self-employment	n.a.	n.a.	n.a.	– 14 200	– 400	1 200	– 300	600

n.a.: Not available.
Note: Most figures are annual averages, while those for 1996 refer to May. However, all data concerning benefit recipients and persons registered for over 3 years refer to December.
Source: NEO (1996).

Table 1.8. **Employment by sector**

Percentage distribution

	1993	1994	1995	1996
Agriculture	**10.7**	**11.6**	**10.5**	**9.9**
Industry	**44.1**	**42.3**	**43.2**	**42.0**
Power, water	1.4	1.1	1.5	1.4
Mining, chemicals	4.5	4.4	4.5	4.2
Metal mfg., engineering	9.2	8.2	7.7	7.5
Other manufacturing	23.6	22.9	24.3	23.5
Construction	5.4	5.6	5.1	5.4
Services	**45.1**	**46.2**	**46.3**	**48.0**
Trade, hotels	14.6	15.0	15.3	15.5
Transport, communications	6.5	6.1	5.9	5.8
Finance, insurance	1.9	2.1	2.3	2.4
Public administration	4.3	4.4	4.4	4.6
Other services	17.7	18.5	18.4	19.5
Total	**100**	**100**	**100**	**100**

Source: LFS data in NSO *Rapid Report* (1995).

(Orazem *et al.*, 1995). The latter figure is similar to the separation rates for industry in Poland, Bulgaria and Romania (17 to 22 per cent in 1993, according to the *Statistical yearbooks*). Many separations are associated with mobility between sectors. According to the LFS, about 7 per cent of those employed in industry in any of the years 1993 to 1995 were working in the service sector one year later, while the flow in the opposite direction was almost as great. In other words, the gross flows were several times greater than the net employment shift from industry to services[9]. In addition, employers hired many persons from among the previously inactive population: about one-fourth of all inactive persons aged 25 to 49 in any year were employed one year later.

One striking effect of Slovenia's transition is that educational attainment has become much more important as a determinant of an individual's employment chances. This is probably part of a long-term trend, as in most countries, but in Slovenia it involved a particularly large and sudden shift in the composition of labour demand, occurring in the early transition phase, as Vodopivec (1996*a*) has shown by analysing labour market flows. Thus, workers who left or lost jobs in 1991 had a 20 per cent chance of being employed again within a month if they had only primary education or less, but about 40 per cent if they had secondary education and over 50 per cent with higher education. In 1987, by contrast, the chances of re-employment within a month were at least about 75 per cent for any educational group[10]. Similarly, for persons who entered unemployment in 1987, the likelihood of finding work within a year was about 60 per cent or higher for most educational groups; whereas, for anyone who became unemployed in 1991, the corresponding job chances had fallen to 40 per cent for persons with only primary education, but remained essentially unchanged for those with higher education.

In the past few years, the workforce has continued to become better educated. The trend may still be driven by demand factors, but it is largely supported by developments on the supply side of the labour market. Among persons in employment, the proportion having less than two years of secondary education fell from 30 per cent in 1994 to 26 per cent in 1996 – a change almost identical to that of the whole labour force, with some educational improvement recorded for the unemployed as well (Table 1.5). But the OECD Secretariat's analysis of a panel of LFS micro-data for 1993 through 1996 suggests that the likelihood of an unemployed person being employed one year later remains somewhat lower for those with only primary education compared with other groups (see below).

In sum, the fall in employment resulting from the transition has been halted, and to a small extent even reversed, although the beginning of 1996 was marked by stagnation. The reallocation of labour continues, with considerable gross flows of workers between sectors. The educational attainment of the employed workforce is increasing; this is due less to upskilling of adults than to the entry of well-educated persons into the labour force and exits by those with poor education. In spite of all these changes, Slovenia's labour market is still characterised by relatively low service-sector employment and a relatively large industrial sector, with many jobs that must be regarded as potentially threatened by further structural change.

Unemployment

Is unemployment high in Slovenia?

Analysing unemployment trends in Slovenia is complicated by the large discrepancy between the two principal data sources: the administrative register of the National Employment Office (NEO) and the LFS.

The most frequently cited statistic is the "registered" unemployment rate, which has been constantly about 14 per cent over the past four years. The figure recorded for May 1996, 118 000 persons or 13.7 per cent of the labour force, surpassed the unemployment rates by any definition in most OECD countries, and was also high compared with many transition countries, although lower than in Poland and Slovakia. (To calculate this rate, the Slovenian authorities use a labour force estimate based on employment data from enterprise surveys. If the registered unemployment is related to the labour force as measured by the LFS, the rate is 12.5 per cent.)

But, as a rule, LFS data are more suitable for international comparison, and they suggest a much lower unemployment rate. Using definitions in line with those of the ILO and Eurostat, the LFS unemployment rate was just over 9 per cent of the labour force in 1993 and 1994, falling to 7.3 per cent in 1995 and 7.4 per cent in 1996. This is comparable with the OECD average of 7.6 per cent for 1995, and well below the 11 per cent average for Western Europe as well as the rates in most transition countries (Chart 1.4). The absolute number of the unemployed was about 70 000 in May 1996. Starting in 1997, Slovenia plans to conduct the LFS every quarter[11].

Why do the two data series give such different unemployment rates? The main explanation, as it appears from the LFS in May 1996, is that the official unemployment register included 55 000 persons who either worked or did not seek work or were not available for it, and therefore were not counted as unemployed according to the international definition (Tables 1.9 and 1.10)[12]. In order to be registered they must in principle seek work, as discussed in Chapter 3, but this is not strictly enforced. About 21 000 of them had some kind of employment, mostly temporary in nature, while 34 000 were not in the labour force according to LFS definitions[13].

Some of these persons regarded themselves as unemployed. In 1996, altogether 32 000 persons – including some who were not even in the NEO's register – regarded themselves as unemployed while being classified as not in the labour force by the LFS (Table 1.6). This may reflect a "discouraged worker" phenomenon, *i.e.* persons who would like to work but have given up active job search. But it is possible that many prefer not to work. In either case, some of the persons concerned are likely to be elderly and *de facto* retired, while others may be youths who have not really entered the labour market.

◆   Chart 1.4.   ***Unemployment according to labour force surveys
in selected transition countries***

Percentage of the labour force

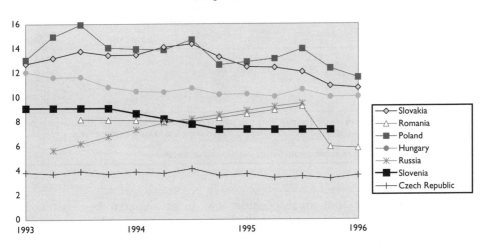

Table 1.9. **Distribution of persons on the NEO's unemployment register according to their replies to the labour force survey, May 1996**

Thousands of registered unemployed persons saying they were:	
Unemployed	**63**
Employed	**21**
Temporary work	4
Other employees	3
Self-employment	2
Family work	4
"Contract work" and related forms of employment	8
Not in the labour force	**34**
Students	2
Retired	0.3
Disabled	4
Housewives	2
"Discouraged": want work but do not seek jobs actively	23
Others	4
Total	**118**

Source: Estimates based on the LFS.

Table 1.10. **Distribution of the working-age population by labour force status: comparison of LFS data with official statistics**

Thousands of persons aged 15 to 64 years, May 1996

The working-age population as classified in official statistics	The working-age population as classified in the LFS			
	Employed	Unemployed	Not in the labour force	Total
Employed	748	0	0	748
Unemployed	21	63	34	118
Not in the labour force	93	7	427	527
Total	862	70	461	1 393

Note: The "official" data sources are the National Statistical Office's enterprise surveys and the NEO's unemployment register. It was assumed that all persons who were employed according to the enterprise surveys were so classified by the LFS as well.
Source: Replies to LFS questions about registration as unemployed at the NEO.

Apparently, many individuals consider it as an advantage to be registered as unemployed, even when they are not eligible for unemployment benefits or other NEO programmes. One reason may be that this facilitates access to pension and health insurance. (The NEO pays insurance contributions for unemployment benefit recipients. Other registered unemployed persons may obtain pension insurance for a fee, and they can apply for free health insurance, which if approved is paid by municipalities.) Moreover, until the summer of 1996, persons who wanted to enrol in adult education had to show that they were either employed or unemployed, but the rules have now been changed in this respect.

More generally, the internationally high labour force participation rate and the low incidence of part-time employment suggest that there cannot be much labour market slack in excess of the LFS-based unemployment rate for the age group 25 to 50. In the age groups under 25 and over 50, by contrast, the potential labour force is evidently greater than the actual one. Hence, for youths and elderly persons, LFS unemployment data may underestimate the full extent of under-employment.

The composition of unemployment

Unemployment is higher for men than for women, but the difference has narrowed in the past four years (Chart 1.5). Between the surveys in 1993 and 1996, the LFS unemployment rate for men fell from 9.9 to 7.5 per cent, while for women it fell from 8.3 to 7 per cent.

The share of first-job seekers in LFS unemployment is about 13 per cent, or 9 000 persons – i.e., less than the 20 per cent share, or 24 000 persons, in the NEO's unemployment register. This implies that the average young Slovene entering the labour market for the first time is unemployed by LFS definitions for about four months, while remaining on the NEO register for almost eleven months[14]. The unemployment rate is much higher for youths than for adults, even according to the LFS; in 1996 it was about 19 per cent for either gender in the age group 15 to 24, compared with 6 per cent in the age group 25 to 49.

In the age group 50 to 64, LFS unemployment is below 4 per cent. This appears to reflect a pattern where persons who lose their jobs after the age of 50 tend to withdraw from active job search – something which, as already seen, does not exclude the possibility that many of them may be registered as unemployed at the NEO. As will be explained in Chapter 3, the maximum duration of unemployment compensation can be extended by up to three additional years as a bridge to retirement.

Persons with low educational attainment are over-represented among the unemployed (Table 1.5). The proportion with under two years of secondary education is tending to fall, but was still 38 per cent of LFS unemployment in 1996, compared with 27 per cent in the whole labour force. Judging from these data, the competitive disadvantage of having only primary education has become more pronounced since 1994. (A given educational group can be considered as disadvantaged if it accounts for a higher share of unemployment than of employment, as shown by a positive difference in the last column for each year in the table.)

◆   Chart 1.5.   **Unemployment rates by gender, age and educational attainment**
Percentage of the labour force

By gender

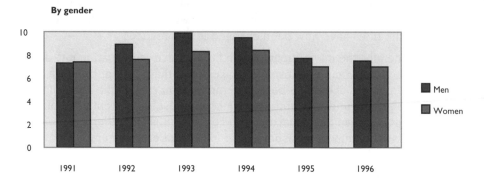

By age

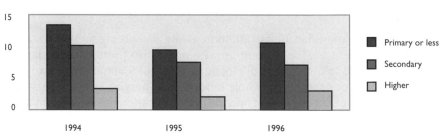

By educational attainment

Note: Estimates for small categories are approximate.
Source: LFS data from NSO *Rapid reports.*

Labour market flows and the duration of unemployment

More than half of the annual inflow of newly unemployed workers to the NEO comes from outside the labour force, being classified either as first-job seekers or as re-entrants to the labour market. Similarly, the 1996 LFS reports that more than half of the stock of unemployment belonged to these two categories, with re-entrants of both genders as the largest group.

The NEO reveals, moreover, that redundancies (*i.e.* permanent lay-offs) accounted for 19 000 new unemployment registrations in 1993, but only 12 000 such cases in 1994 and fewer than 10 000 in 1995. In contrast, more workers have become unemployed as a result of the termination of temporary jobs: 14 000 in 1993, 15 000 in 1994 and over 20 000 in 1995.

Data on flows out of unemployment suggest that the job chances faced by unemployed people have worsened since 1993. Thus, according to the

Table 1.11. **Probabilities of transition between labour-force situations**

A. Flows between May 1993 and May 1994 as a percentage of the stock in May 1993

Labour force status in 1993	Labour force status in 1994			
	Employed	Unemployed	Not in the labour force	Total
Employed	91	3	6	100
Unemployed	42	43	15	100
Not in the labour force	9	3	88	100

B. Flows between May 1994 and May 1995 as a percentage of the stock in May 1994

Labour force status in 1994	Labour force status in 1995			
	Employed	Unemployed	Not in the labour force	Total
Employed	92	2	6	100
Unemployed	39	42	19	100
Not in the labour force	10	3	87	100

C. Flows between May 1995 and May 1996 as a percentage of the stock in May 1995

Labour force status in 1995	Labour force status in 1996			
	Employed	Unemployed	Not in the labour force	Total
Employed	90	3	7	100
Unemployed	36	42	22	100
Not in the labour force	9	3	88	100

Source: LFS panel data. Figures for 1996 are provisional.

Secretariat's analysis of LFS micro-data, the likelihood that an average unemployed person would have work one year later (*i.e.* at the time of the next survey) was 42 per cent in 1993, but only 36 per cent for those who were unemployed in May 1995 (Table 1.11). Persons with only primary education were somewhat less likely than others to move into employment.

A smaller but possibly increasing proportion had left the labour force one year later. This was the case with about one-fifth of those unemployed at the time of the 1995 LFS, with a somewhat higher share of women than men, but little difference between educational groups.

Long-term unemployment is substantial, but has fallen since a peak in 1994, according to both available data sources. The incidence of long-term (over 12 months) in total unemployment in 1994 was 59 per cent according to the LFS and 62 per cent according to the NEO. By May 1996, this share was 52 per cent according to the LFS, while a sample of NEO files drawn in June 1996 suggests that it was 56 per cent. It can also be estimated – from LFS micro-data – that 47 per cent of all unemployment spells that were completed during the past three years had lasted for over a year.

Unemployment lasting longer than two years has also become less common, according to the LFS (one-third of the unemployment stock in 1996). But the NEO, by contrast, reported a continued increase in very long-term unemployment, at least until the end of 1995, when 25 per cent of the registered unemployed had been so for over three years. About 8 per cent (10 000 persons) had been on the register for over five years.

CONCLUSIONS

Labour market conditions seem to have been largely favourable to new business and job creation, in spite of the fact that the new jobs often require higher qualifications than the ones they replace. However, a significant proportion of the new jobs are temporary in nature, including most probably an element of "grey-market" employment that is difficult to assess. This may indicate that some employers regard the standard forms of employment contract as too rigid, or otherwise as ill-suited to their situation.

But the economic transition has destroyed many jobs. The negative impact on employment has been small for the "prime-age" group of 25 to 49, but substantial for youths and those aged over 50. As in many countries, labour force participation has fallen to low levels for these two groups. With regard to the middle-aged and elderly, a major policy issue concerns the low average retirement age, which will be discussed in Chapter 4. The problems at stake here are not only the pension costs and the loss of potential output. A low average retirement age can also reduce incentives for adults to engage in work-oriented education and training; instead, it may encourage middle-aged workers, even in low-paid jobs, to behave defensively, often preferring, if possible, to stay where they are until retirement.

Even more troubling, perhaps, is that many young people who entered the labour market in recent years have no complete secondary education. Low-qualified persons are often out of work, and there is a risk that they will continue to be in a vulnerable position for many years. A sustained policy effort to promote adult education, not least for persons with low initial education, would therefore seem required. With respect to future age classes of labour market entrants, it is too early to determine if the current educational reforms, including the apprenticeship system, will be sufficient to reduce the size of the group with no qualifications.

There may also be reason for concern with the generally low labour force participation rate reported for youths under age 25. This may be partly explained by the high rate of enrolment in post-secondary education, which itself can be justified. However, comparisons between OECD countries suggest that longer initial education may be most likely to help the youngsters find work if they have some contact with the labour market during the years of study. (This may be achieved either by occasional stints of temporary or part-time work, as is relatively common among students in Denmark, the Netherlands and most English-speaking countries, or by participation in education of the apprenticeship type, as in Austria and Germany. See OECD, 1996d, Table B.) Where this is less common, as in most Mediterranean OECD countries, unemployment is often substantial even among those with relatively high educational qualifications. As far as Slovenia is concerned, it appears justified in this perspective to preserve, and perhaps further improve, the country's present system for placing students in temporary jobs, as well as its peculiar form of traineeships ("internships").

2

LABOUR RESTRUCTURING IN ENTERPRISES

Slovenia's industrial modernisation is well under way and has shown positive results, for example in terms of higher productivity and falling unit labour costs, but many companies are still unprofitable. Following the substantial reductions of output, employment and wages during the initial transition period until 1992, developments have been characterised by moderate wage increases and a continued, but largely undramatic, reallocation of labour. Small enterprises and non-traditional forms of employment have grown at the expense of permanent employment in large firms, several of which are still faced by unresolved structural problems.

The privatisation of large enterprises, implemented after frequent delays, needs to be followed up by further restructuring in many firms. This chapter will consider the institutional prerequisites, focusing especially on the ways in which privatisation was achieved, the wage-setting system, the cost to employers of making workers redundant and the use of subsidies to industry. It would appear that public policy interventions in these areas have tended to favour a cautious approach to restructuring. Some policies with such effects may be justified for various reasons, but taken together they do not necessarily provide the optimal combination of restrictions and opportunities for business. In a long-term perspective, labour market policy is most effective if it facilitates the necessary labour adjustments. The need for restructuring is still great, as is indicated by the size of the operating losses incurred by Slovenian enterprises in 1994 and 1995.

The chapter will first examine some general information about enterprises, followed by a section devoted to privatisation. It then considers industrial relations, wage-setting, recruitment and employment security provisions. Lastly, it briefly reviews some indicators of the results achieved to date in terms of restructuring.

THE SIZE OF FIRMS IN INDUSTRY AND SERVICES

The total number of active enterprises, including those without employees, increased from about 4 000 in 1989 to 33 600 in 1995 (according to the Agency for Payments Transactions; see *Slovenian Business Report*, 1996). But only 18 firms employed over 2 000 persons in 1995. The largest firms were the state railways (9 700 employees), the clothing manufacturer Mura (6 000) and the postal service (5 100). Other firms with more than 2 000 employees included producers of coal, household appliances, cars, pharmaceuticals and tyres, and the telecommunications company.

At the other end of the spectrum, small firms have proliferated, especially in services but also in industry. About 30 000 enterprises in the commercial sector had fewer than 250 employees in 1995, but they accounted for only 40 per cent of the total employment in commercial enterprises (some 20 per cent of total employment according to the LFS). To this must be added about 50 000 self-employed "craftsmen", each with on average one employee, thus representing about 100 000 employed persons (11 per cent of total employment), up from about 70 000 in 1990. Many businesses of both types are run by self-employed persons without employees.

Apart from agriculture, about 13 000 commercial enterprises had paid employees in 1995, of which 11 000 were in the service sector and 2 200 in industry. In the service sector, over half of the enterprises with employees had fewer than seven persons on the payroll, while only a few hundred firms had over 125 employees. Among the industrial enterprises, some 530 had more than 125 employees, while about 80 firms had more than 500 (Statistical Yearbook, 1995).

At the aggregate level, there has been a shift in employment from industry to the service sector, as noted in Chapter 1. Within industry, the contraction has occurred especially in metal manufacturing and engineering, and also in mining, while other manufacturing sectors have seen a modest net increase in employment.

PRIVATISATION

The only private businesses that existed under the previous system were the "craftsmen", whose numbers including employees, as already mentioned, increased by some 50 per cent, or by 30 000, between 1989 and 1995. Their activities can be more varied than the term suggests. More important than this increase, however, was the fact that the creation of formal enterprises was liberalised in 1989, setting in motion a wave of small business start-ups creating about 90 000 jobs by 1994, corresponding to 19 per cent of employment in commercial enterprises in the latter year[15]. About 90 per cent of all commercial enterprises with under 50 employees were then private, but they employed on average only two workers. Altogether, according to an estimate by the Agency for Restructuring and Privatisation, the private-sector share of GDP surpassed 40 per cent by 1994, or about as much as the "socially-owned" sector (public authorities accounting for the remaining 15 per cent of GDP). This implies that the private sector in 1994 was still smaller in relative terms than the 55 per cent recorded in Poland and Hungary, but similar to the situation at that time in Slovakia (IAMD, 1996b; Brada, 1996; Podkaminer, 1995).

The privatisation of "socially-owned" businesses, still numbering about 1 500 in 1994, occurred essentially in 1995 and 1996 after a period of uncertainty about various legal and economic issues. In theory, these firms belonged to all citizens, but there was no specific procedure by which the government could exercise ownership rights; in effect, they were controlled by their managers and employees. Before privatisation could occur, it was therefore necessary to establish a legal framework, administered by the newly established Agency for Restructuring and Privatisation, and another state-controlled body that could act as a temporary owner if necessary: the Development Fund.

The process was initiated by a 1992 Law on Ownership Transformation of Companies, accompanied by a Company Law, a Bankruptcy Law, a Restitution Law and a host of other regulations (Jaklin, 1995). All "socially-owned" firms were obliged to establish the value of their capital and prepare a plan for its transfer to "known owners", *i.e.* shareholders, whose rights were henceforth defined for joint-stock and limited-liability companies. Two key approvals had to be obtained from the Agency for Restructuring and Privatisation. First, each enterprise had to submit a proposal specifying the chosen methods for distribution of shares, accompanied by a balance sheet and information about restructuring measures to be taken before privatisation. Most firms did so shortly before an official deadline at the end of 1994. Once the Agency had approved such a proposal, with possible changes, the company must implement it and obtain the Agency's final approval, which is a condition for registration in the Court Register of Companies. On 15 November 1996, over 1 300 companies had obtained the Agency's initial plan approval, while 171 firms had still to reach this stage. Final approval had been awarded to 780 enterprises, while applications from a further 133 firms were under consideration by the Agency. About 30 firms were wholly owned by the Development Fund and as many had gone bankrupt.

This privatisation programme concerned companies accounting for roughly half of Slovenia's employment, 45 per cent of the enterprise capital and 40 per cent of the income, but it did not cover banks, insurance companies and public utilities (IMAD, 1996*b*, pp. 3-6). Each citizen received non-transferable vouchers worth 100 000 to 400 000 Tolars, depending on his or her age, to be used for buying "social" equity in the companies where they were employed or in other companies, but not for other purposes[16]. Together, these vouchers initially amounted to 40 per cent of the book value of all such equity at the end of 1992.

As a rule, 20 per cent of each company's capital must be transferred free of charge to the Development Fund, for subsequent sale to authorised Special Investment Funds which must be private, and an additional 20 per cent to two other state-controlled funds. The remaining 60 per cent of the shares must be sold, for vouchers or money, and here the companies could choose between different approaches[17]. Proceeds go to the Development Fund. The large majority of firms have sold shares to their own employees, who are entitled to buy 40 per cent of the stock at a 50 per cent discount and a further 20 per cent at the full price, in the latter case with an obligation to keep the shares for two years.

In August 1996, insiders owned 36 per cent of the combined value of the privatised firms. Funds owned 34 per cent, small investors 12 per cent and others 18 per cent (including restitution beneficiaries and foreign owners). This situation is likely to give insiders effective control of most firms, since the public funds probably do not have sufficient staff resources to participate in many board meetings or other forms of supervision. According to Jaklin (1995), over 80 per cent of the companies privatised in 1995 avoided selling any shares to outsiders other than the public funds. Foreign ownership, in particular, was often strongly opposed.

Surveys by the Agency have indicated that many shareholders, especially among the insiders, want profits to be re-invested rather than paid out as dividends, and a majority do not seem to intend to sell their shares. Shares in large companies may gradually become more widely traded in the future, however. Turnover at the Ljubljana Stock Exchange and the OTC (over-the-counter) was five times greater in 1995 than in any previous year (about 600 billion Tolars, with a market capitalisation of about 100 billion). The foreign direct investment remains modest, accounting for a capital inflow of about 21 billion Tolars in 1995, but there is evidence that foreign-owned firms are among the best performers within several industries (IMAD, 1996b, p. 6).

The Development Fund, for its part, sells its share holdings as soon as it can to Special Investment Funds, in which the public can buy shares in exchange for privatisation vouchers. Most of these funds are controlled by banks. Their operations are in the hands of authorised fund management and investment companies, expected to focus on economic performance. But their capacity to play an active role in running companies is probably limited, and they have not brought much fresh capital into the companies.

INDUSTRIAL RELATIONS AND WAGE SETTING

Institutional arrangements

Wages have been subject to collective bargaining since 1991, contrary to the previous system, in which the government essentially determined the wage bill for each enterprise. Nevertheless, the government continues to be involved in the process. Several detailed practices relating to actual wage outcomes as well as procedural matters are only gradually being changed. It is therefore pertinent to consider the key features of the previous wage-setting system before turning to the present situation[18].

When Slovenia was part of Yugoslavia, the government of the republic sought to control the overall wage costs and their distribution between companies through "agreements" with the "self-management" bodies. In the late 1980s, this involved the calculation of indicators of business success for each firm, taking account of its revenues per worker and per capital unit[19]. These indicators were evened out between firms in such a way that, in typical cases, less than half of the variation in business success was allowed to influence the wage costs. The resulting "socially warranted" wage bills were then imposed on enterprises, their financing being assured by a more or less equivalent redistribution of enterprise revenue by means of taxes, subsidies, forced loans and large negative returns to capital. Once a firm's wage bill had been determined, the wage scale was decided by referendum among its employees, following a common pattern with education as the main basis for differentiation. Other individual factors, such as job tenure and performance, were less important in fixing wages for individual employees. In large firms, the ratio between the highest and the lowest wage could be about 4 to 1.

The 1991 Labour Law makes collective agreements the principal instrument for wage setting. But the government still plays a strong role, imposing a top-down bargaining model. Although it is not compulsory to sign collective agreements at company level, the rules have resulted in a practice of multi-tier bargaining, where national wage increases are topped up by further increases agreed upon at industry and company level.

Collective agreements at national level are compulsory: if no agreement had been signed, the previous wage scale would have continued to have legal force. The law assumes as a rule that agreements are intended to have general validity in the labour market areas covered. Once signed, a collective agreement is legally binding. It must be published and registered by the authorities, but these cannot impose changes in their content. (The Labour Ministry registers national agreements; municipalities register company agreements.) A new Law on Collective Agreements and a new Labour Relations Law are under preparation, however, and they are expected to limit an agreement's automatic validity to the signatory parties. Even so, if the employers represent more than half of a sector's employment, and if the trade unions represent more than half of their workforce, they will probably become entitled to obtain, on demand, a declaration by the Labour Minister to the effect that their agreement has general validity. (Such a possibility exists in several OECD countries[20].)

Two main collective agreements are in force, one for the commercial and one for the non-commercial sector. They run for two or three years, with wage scales renewed annually, and are signed by several trade unions and the Chamber of Commerce, which represents employers by virtue of compulsory membership. A new voluntary "Employers' Association of Slovenia" also takes part in the bargaining. Public-sector collective agreements, following the same rules, are signed by the government on the employer side. Civil servants have no special status, but may obtain this as a result of legislation now being prepared. Currently, only judges and members of Parliament have special provisions.

Each trade union must be registered by the Ministry of Labour, Family and Social Affairs, which also determines which of them can represent the workers at national and sectoral level. As a rule, according to a Law on Representativity of Trade Unions, a union can be declared representative if it represents 15 per cent of the workforce in a sector. Since 1993, the Ministry has registered four confederations and 130 other trade unions (of which many belong to the confederations). A status of national representativity has been recognised in the case of the four confederations, ten sectoral and eight occupational associations. No systematic information is available about their membership, apart from the fact that it was found to exceed the required 15 per cent in the cases when they were declared representative.

From 1994, the government has also stepped in to establish a national framework for wage setting – as the governments did before the transition, though in different forms. This has led to annual "Social Agreements", signed by the government and the main trade union and employer associations, including some that represent small firms. The government, which initiated the process, was concerned with the need to prevent social unrest in the transition and with the risk of inflationary wage increases. As a complement, the Parliament imposed a cap on wages in 1994 and 1995, but this was not considered to be very effective; in 1996, it was replaced by a tax-based incomes policy.

The 1994 Agreement also created a permanent tripartite institution, the Social and Economic Council, with a revolving chairmanship and a permanent secretariat. It serves as a forum for consultation on economic and social policy issues, and it assists in formulating the Social Agreements and in their implementation and monitoring. Since 1995, the Social Agreements have treated several economic policy questions in addition to the wage issues.

The 1996 Agreement (see Box 2) introduced a progressive payroll tax, combined with a 4 per cent cut in social security contributions and a rule that real wages should increase by 2 percentage points less than GDP during the year. It generally endorsed the government's intention to reduce public spending; but it promised a continued role for temporary subsidies to preserve jobs – albeit only on the condition that they can become viable in the long term – together with interest subsidies for investments and support of technological development. It also called for some measures which appear difficult to reconcile with a policy of international economic integration, such as a public procurement policy to favour local suppliers – except when this is prohibited by international agreements – and "non-customs protection of the economy". The precise nature of these measures was not specified in the Agreement, however.

A Labour Inspectorate, with about 70 inspectors, and a system of labour and social courts are in place to enforce labour law and collective agreements, including the Social Agreement. The inspectors notably check that wages do not fall below the minimum rate. Official monitoring is facilitated by the fact that most payments still go through the Agency for Payments Transactions, which automatically checks for some forms of abuse, deducts taxes and produces statistics. But it is no longer compulsory for enterprises to use this agency for payments, and from 1997 most of its legal control functions have been taken over by the tax authorities. Small firms increasingly use banks, which must report to the latter.

Box 2. **The 1996 Social Agreement**

The Agreement lays down the key objectives for 1996, including a 5 per cent GDP growth, lower inflation than in 1995, a more efficient transition of unemployed people into jobs, and a reduction in the weight of public finance in GDP.

A principal goal is to preserve real pay without increasing unit labour costs. More specifically:

- The employers' social security contributions are cut from 42 to 38 per cent of the wages. Instead, a tax-based incomes policy is introduced, in the shape of a progressive payroll tax. (The Social Agreement envisaged a zero payroll tax rate for monthly incomes of up to 85 000 Tolars, and a ceiling rate of 6 per cent from 750 000 Tolars. Subsequently, the Parliament has fixed slightly higher income limits and increased the top rate to 10 per cent.) Taken together, these two measures were expected to reduce labour costs by 1.6 per cent. It was agreed to follow this up during the next two years by measures involving a further 2.4 per cent cut in labour costs.

- As a target, real-wage growth in the commercial sector should be 2 percentage points below the current year's real GDP growth. Agreed "base" wages are to be adjusted every three months by 85 per cent of the increase in retail prices over the last quarter.

- Loss-making firms and those with liquidity problems can negotiate lower adjustment rates with their unions, but they cannot pay less than the minimum wage. For executive staff, the three-monthly wage adjustments are made only in firms that have been privatised.

- Firms in the commercial sector pay an annual holiday bonus of 102 000 Tolars, or, if business results permit, one month's wage.

- In addition, profitable companies may pay an extra amount of up to one monthly wage, though not more than 25 per cent of the profit.

- The minimum wage was fixed at 53 500 Tolars per month for the second quarter (about 45 per cent of the average wage), subject to the same quarterly adjustments as other wages. For the future, it was agreed that the minimum wage should be regulated by law, taking account of the country's economic development.

- The government shall propose measures to make the Labour Inspectorate more effective, especially with regard to illegal employment.

Wages

The main collective agreement for the commercial sector specifies "base" wages for 24 industries and nine educational levels. These are updated quarterly to take account of inflation, as regulated in the Social Agreement. In any industry, the ratio between base wages for the highest and the lowest educational category is about 3.5 to 1. Most job types fall under one of the nine educational categories, but the base wages can be adjusted upwards to form "individual basic" wages, using coefficients, up to no more than the next higher education step.

These base wages serve as a floor for further bargaining. Higher wages and additional rights are normally established at industry level. Thereafter, a third-tier collective agreement can be negotiated at the enterprise level, with more upward differentiation according to individual job classifications. The wage increases agreed upon in companies vary according to their profitability. In addition, as envisaged in the Social Agreement, enterprises can pay up to 25 per cent of their profits as a bonus, usually as a 13th monthly wage. In total, therefore, the compensation package for a worker can include twelve monthly wages, a holiday bonus and a year-end bonus based on the preliminary operating surplus of the firm.

The minimum wage specified in the Social Agreement, 53 500 Tolars in May 1996, applies to the monthly wages excluding any year-end bonus. Enterprises facing economic distress have previously been allowed, in collective agreements, to pay 20 per cent less than the base wages, but this downward flexibility was limited to 5 per cent by the 1995 and 1996 agreements, and wages must in any case not be lower than the minimum wage. A survey by the NSO in March 1996 (i.e. before the 1996 agreements were signed) found that about 1 per cent of all full-time employees then received the minimum wage or less.

In the non-commercial sector, the main collective agreement specifies a base wage for the lowest educational level, to be multiplied by coefficients ranging from 1.1 to 3 for the other eight educational levels. In addition, in 1996, the base wages at the four lowest levels are multiplied by up to 1.15, a measure intended to reduce a wage differential relative to the commercial sector. Public employers in the non-commercial sector (i.e. the bulk of this sector) must also take account of a second set of coefficients laid down in law[21], ranging from 1 to 4 for most job types, but stretching up to 9 for senior positions. The law distinguishes several sub-categories of posts within each educational category, and permits wage adjustments for good performance and special conditions, within a limit of 20 per cent for an individual and 3 per cent for an employer. There are also new possibilities for advancement. In practice, the coefficients fixed by law apply in the higher grades, where they exceed those of the collective agreement, while the opposite is true at lower levels. On average, because of a relatively high average educational attainment, before-tax wages in 1995 were 28 per cent higher than in the commercial sector. Preliminary information for 1996 suggests that this difference between the sectors has increased.

More generally, wage differentials based on educational attainment have widened in the transition period, especially during its early phase, as documented by Vodopivec (1996a). Jobs requiring a university degree paid on average twice the mean wage in 1994, up from 180 per cent in 1990. Some groups of management staff have obtained substantially greater increases, based on individual contracts which cover some 3 per cent of the workforce. At the other end, unskilled workers earned only 59 per cent of the mean wage, down from 68 per cent in 1990[22].

In most respects, however, wage differentials have remained relatively small. If 11 broad sectors are considered, the average wages in 1995 varied in relative terms from 1 to 1.7[23], while the averages for the 24 industries identified in the main collective agreement for the commercial sector fell in the range of 1 to 2.5. Comparing local communities, the highest average wages in 1993 (in Ljubljana centre, Bezigrad and Piran) were about 20 per cent above the national average, which in turn was about 25 per cent higher than the lowest community average (in Sevnica). Women working full-time earned on average 14 per cent less than men (*Statistical Yearbook*, 1995).

Overall, the average gross wages in 1995 (116 000 Tolars per month before tax, or almost $1 000) remained about 6 per cent lower in real terms than they were in 1990, while after-tax wages had increased by 8 per cent (Chart 2.1). These trend figures conceal some exceptionally strong real-wage fluctuations associated with hyperinflation, culminating in 1989 and continuing until 1992. Thus, the real-wage drop in 1991 – by about one-third from December to December after tax, or slightly

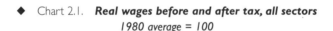

◆   Chart 2.1.   **Real wages before and after tax, all sectors**
1980 average = 100

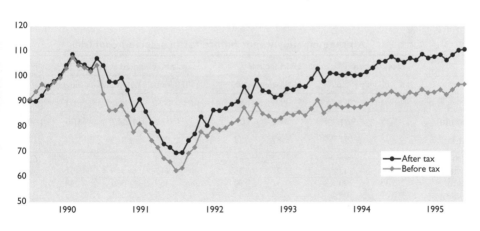

Note: Monthly wages were compared at the consumer price level of December 1995.
Source: *Statistical Yearbook* (1996) and submissions from NSO.

more before tax – was followed by a similarly large increase in 1992[24]. In 1993 to 1995, the real-wage growth was between 3 and 7 per cent per year, both before and after tax. During 1996, real wages first fell briefly before the collective agreements for the year had been signed, but a relatively strong increase seems to have occurred thereafter, notwithstanding the cautious approach taken in the Social Agreement (IMAD, 1996a)[25].

At current exchange rates, the average wage in 1995 was at least three times higher than in the Czech Republic, Hungary, Poland or Slovakia (Table 2.1). However, this difference is explained in part by the fact that the Tolar is relatively over-valued. (Its dollar value even increased by 8 per cent between 1994 and 1995.) In terms of purchasing power parities (PPPs), the wage level in Slovenia is 1.7 times as high as in the Czech Republic and two to four times as high as in other Central and Eastern European countries. It is also notable that the average wage in 1995 corresponded to 120 per cent of the per capita GDP, *i.e.* slightly more than in Poland (114 per cent) and much more than in the Czech Republic (82 per cent, 1994), Hungary (86 per cent), and the Slovak Republic (91 per cent).

In sum, real wages in Slovenia are relatively high and their dispersion remains moderate, although it has widened. The government's role in wage setting appears as very active if all the above-mentioned policy instruments are taken into account, *i.e.* the Social Agreements, the tax-based income policies, the law that makes national agreements compulsory and the registration procedure for trade unions and collective agreements. This array of policy interventions may have been justified in a transition phase, but in the long run it would arguably be better if employers and workers could fulfil their responsibilities more independently of the government.

Table 2.1. **Average monthly wages before tax in selected countries**

	Wages compared at current exchange rates				Wages compared at PPPs			
	U.S. dollars per month		Slovenia = 100		U.S. dollars per month		Slovenia = 100	
	1994	1995	1994	1995	1994	1995	1994	1995
Slovenia	**735**	**961**	**100**	**100**	**1 010**	**1 067**	**100**	**100**
Austria	2 696	3 191	367	332	2 215	2 315	219	217
Czech Republic	232	296	32	31	594	645	59	60
Slovakia	196	242	27	25	512	549	51	51
Poland	235	290	32	30	489	520	48	49
Hungary	317	309	43	32	355	371	35	35
Bulgaria	73	106	10	11	342	350	34	33
Romania	86	104	12	11	254	286	25	27

Source: OECD.

EMPLOYMENT PROTECTION AND RECRUITMENT PRACTICES

Until 1989, employees could generally not be dismissed for economic reasons unless the employer went bankrupt. The situation changed little after the first round of reforms decided at federal level, because the new lay-off rules initially required a notice period of 24 months. But Slovenia shortened this requirement to 6 months in 1991, and thereafter the majority of separations initiated by employers have been ordinary redundancies rather than the result of bankruptcies.

Redundancies can be relatively expensive to employers. In addition to the wages pertaining to the notification period, workers with a tenure of more than two years are entitled to a severance payment corresponding to half a month's wages for every year of service. However, contrary to the rules in most countries, the employers may reduce the wages paid during the notification period by 30 per cent, though not below the minimum wage, if the workers are sent home. Employers can also pay the whole amount as a lump-sum, usually with a smaller wage reduction.

In other countries, the corresponding redundancy costs to employers are typically lower. For example, the required severance pay is generally two months' wages in the Czech Republic and three in Poland; the notification periods are three months in the Czech Republic and Russia, but less in most other transition countries. In the European Union, severance pay is usually lower than in Slovenia in all countries except Italy; the notification periods are also mostly shorter, but paid at the normal wage rate (OECD, 1995*a* and *b*; OECD, 1994, Table 6.5).

The 1989 legislation, still in force with amendments, assumes that the employers will take active measures to find new jobs or other solutions for the workers they declare redundant. During the 6-month notice period, individual adjustment measures can be partly subsidised by the NEO ("co-financed", often at a rate of 50 per cent). Especially in the period 1991-93, the NEO helped employers purchase additional pension rights for about 13 000 redundant workers, while training was organised in this manner for about 25 000 workers. In the most recent years, such co-financing has been limited to training, and the number of workers concerned has fallen to a few thousand per year (cf. Chapters 3 and 4).

In other respects, however, Slovenia's employment protection legislation is comparatively liberal. Provided that employers follow the required procedures, they are free to declare workers redundant when their labour "for urgent operational reasons" is no longer required (Law on Labour Relations). They must notify the National Employment Office (NEO) as soon as the decision has been taken; if many workers are concerned, they must also propose measures to deal with the situation together with the trade unions[26]. Collective agreements stipulate in general terms that the selection of workers for dismissal should be based on economic and social factors, *i.e.* their productivity as well as their family situation. In practice, employers can generally select the workers they want to dismiss, apart from some groups which cannot be made redundant, *e.g.*, single parents with children under two years of age, older workers and the disabled[27]. Moreover, regardless of the situation of the enterprise, individual factors such as poor performance can also justify dismissal, but only on condition that suitable transfer possibilities do not exist or are refused by the worker.

In the early 1990s, the government usually subsidised the wages during the notification period (in addition to the subsidies for training and early retirement). This is still done in the case of state-owned enterprises, including those wholly owned by the Development Fund, *i.e.* enterprises at risk of going bankrupt, or otherwise difficult to privatise. However, as will be seen in Chapter 3, the largest enterprise subsidies in recent years have been paid, instead, to encourage unprofitable enterprises to keep their workforce. Another possible way for enterprises to reduce restructuring costs is to seek bankruptcy: bankrupt firms do not have to honour the 6-month notification requirement. The number of workers becoming unemployed as a result of bankruptcies has increased somewhat in the past few years, reaching 7 300 in 1995.

The cost of declaring redundancies may also contribute to a widespread use of temporary employment contracts, accounting for about 60 per cent of all job vacancies declared in 1995 (see Chapter 3). Temporary contracts can be legally justified on various grounds, mainly depending on the nature of the work to be done. There is no particular limit to their duration, and they can be renewed. Employers also continue to use traineeships (also called internships), a form of temporary employment contract inherited from Yugoslavia, which serve as the standard port of entry into many careers after secondary or higher education.

For workers in loss-making firms, the best option is often to begin seeking a new job as soon as possible. This is encouraged by the wage scales, which, as seen above, are structured within firms as a function of formal education – *i.e.*, they depend largely on general skills which are easy to document – while they can vary between firms as a function of profitability. Persons with marketable qualifications have good chances of improving their earnings by moving to more profitable firms, as reflected in the observed patterns of labour mobility during the transition (Orazem *et al.*, 1995). On the other hand, if a worker quits a job against the desire of the employer and then fails to find a new one, he or she receives no unemployment benefit – a penalty rule that appears rather strict by international standards. This may discourage job quits by persons who are not so attractive in the labour market (see Chapter 3).

Enterprises that recruit workers seem to face relatively favourable labour market conditions in Slovenia. Business surveys have suggested that employers often consider the availability of labour and its qualifications as a competitive advantage for the country, in spite of the relatively high wages[28]. Recruitments are achieved predominantly through private information channels, with newspapers playing a notable role (apart from personal contacts, which are most important in Slovenia, as elsewhere). According to the LFS, the proportion of all hires in dependent employment resulting from newspaper advertisements was about 18 per cent in the past few years, but increased to 22 per cent in 1996. The proportion rises to about one-half if one disregards vacancies filled by direct or indirect personal contacts. The role of the NEO appears less important by comparison; however, the NEO also advertises vacancies in newspapers (see Chapter 3).

FIRST RESULTS OF LABOUR RESTRUCTURING IN INDUSTRY

Industrial employment has probably declined each year since 1986, although, as discussed in Chapter 1, available statistics are not reliable on this point. According to employer surveys (which understate the growth of new small firms), industrial firms with three or more workers, excluding construction, employed about 250 000 persons in 1994, down from more than 370 000 in the late 1980s (*Statistical Yearbook*, 1995, Table 12.3). If all commercial enterprises are taken into account, the corresponding reduction was from about 650 000 to about 450 000. Many difficult industrial problems have yet to be addressed, as indicated by the fact that some 170 000 employees were in loss-making enterprises in 1995.

Some 120 000 workers lost their jobs involuntarily as a result of structural change in the period 1990 to 1995, if all economic sectors are included (Orazem *et al.*, 1995, Table 2; NEO annual reports). About one-half of this total resulted from bankruptcies, the other half consisting of redundancies according to the rules described above. All displacements occurring before 1991 were due to bankruptcies; they concerned between 500 and 2 000 workers per year in the late 1980s, about 10 000 in 1990 and 19 000 in 1991, declining subsequently to under 10 000 per year. From 1992 on, most of them followed the new redundancy procedures, which covered about 19 000 persons in 1993, but fewer than 10 000 in 1995.

Altogether, these two types of involuntary displacement represented about 30 per cent of all job separations in the years 1991 to 1993, falling to about 20 per cent thereafter. Voluntary departures, including most retirements, thus accounted for more than two-thirds of the separations. But some of those who obtained early retirement can be regarded as having been *de facto* displaced, even if they were not formally dismissed at the employer's initiative (see Chapter 4).

What happened to the workers? In a study of persons leaving jobs in 1990, Orazem *et al.* (1995) found, first, that those with above-average education more often left their jobs voluntarily and found new ones, thus avoiding dismissal. Second, among those who were dismissed in 1990 (always by bankruptcy, at the time), one-third had jobs again in 1992, while one-half were still unemployed and the rest had left the labour force. About one-third of those who had jobs earned less than previously, the dismissed workers being more likely than others to experience a loss in income.

For enterprises, job cuts have permitted an improvement in productivity, starting about 1993. Until then, the fall in output had been roughly as great as the fall in employment at the aggregate level, *i.e.* about one-third, but subsequently the output has grown while employment continued to fall (Table 2.2). Output per employee surpassed the 1989 level from 1994 on (although total industrial output is still lower than before the transition). Output per hour of work increased by 12 per cent between 1993 and 1995, a growth trend comparable to that in Hungary, though not as fast as in Poland.

Real producer wages (*i.e.* wages deflated by product prices) fell sharply in 1991, but subsequently increased and by 1995 they had recovered to 88 per cent of the 1989 level, or 93 per cent of the 1990 level (Chart 2.2). Combined with productivity developments, this led to a 20 per cent reduction of real unit labour costs by 1992, partly offset in 1993 by a recovery in real producer wages. In 1994 and 1995, improved productivity and moderate real-wage growth were sufficient to contain real unit labour costs at about 85 per cent of the 1990 level. Chemicals and food-processing industries appear to have become most profitable on average.

However, as already indicated, Slovenian industry as a whole continued to incur large losses in 1995, notably in the paper, machine-building, metal-processing, and electric-power industries. Among a total of over 33 600 registered companies, almost 10 000 reported losses. Almost 80 per cent of the losses concerned large- and medium-sized firms, mainly in industry (IMAD, 1996b).

Evidently, the availability of government subsidies has been one factor that enabled enterprises to sustain heavy losses, although some types of subsidies

Table 2.2. **Changes in productivity and labour costs in industry**

| | Index: 1989 = 100 | | | | | |
	1990	1991	1992	1993	1994	1995
Productivity (output per employee)	96	91	87	93	104	110
Real producer wage	94	71	66	78	84	88
Real unit labour cost[1]	98	78	75	84	81	80
Memorandum items concerning industry:						
Dependent employment (adm. records)	93	86	78	71	68	65
Output volume	89	78	68	66	70	72
Producer prices	490	1 099	3 470	4 233	4 995	5 634
Nominal wages	461	777	2 284	3 307	4 201	4 974

1. The ratio of real producer wages to labour productivity.
Note: The figures refer to mining, manufacturing and electricity supply.
Source: *Statistical Yearbooks* (1994 and 1995).

◆　Chart 2.2.　**Real wages in industry, before tax**
1990 = 100

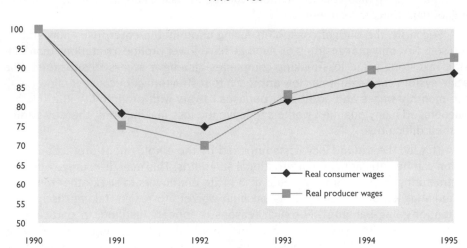

Note:　Average wages were deflated by price indices for consumers and producers, respectively.
Source:　*Statistical Yearbooks* (1994 and 1996).

have been scaled down. During 1995, the Ministry of Labour, Family and Social Affairs and the NEO paid about 5 billion Tolars in subsidies to enterprises, an amount which was expected to fall to about 3 billion Tolars in 1996 (see Chapter 3). The NEO's enterprise subsidy programmes, which generally target individual workers, account for a modest share of this spending.

CONCLUSIONS

The initial conditions for enterprises in Slovenia were more favourable in some respects than in other transition countries. Companies already had experience of competition in product markets in the former Yugoslavia and abroad. The workforce was relatively well educated, and many workers also had experience of working abroad.

Important segments of the Slovenian industry have been able to capitalise on these advantages, but the picture remains mixed at aggregate level. A number of problems continue to slow down the necessary restructuring. This suggests that several public policies may require further fine-tuning and that some types of intervention should be reduced.

First, the widespread insider control of privatised enterprises is likely, on average, to exercise a conservative influence on business decisions related to restructuring. To balance this influence, additional policy measures would seem justified to open the economy to more outside financing and shareholding, including foreign direct investment.

Secondly, the budget constraints facing unprofitable enterprises may still be too soft. Not only may insiders on average have lower profit expectations than outside investors, some loss-making companies also have access to subsidies. The wage system can facilitate a slow approach to restructuring, because it allows both the monthly wages and additional bonuses to vary with profitability. But this has encouraged many qualified workers to leave the loss-making firms, thereby adding to their difficulties.

Thirdly, the redundancy costs imposed by the employment protection legislation can be substantial by international standards. This may discourage effective restructuring in some firms. It could also incite employers to seek other means of terminating employment, such as pushing workers to resign, taking disciplinary action, or going bankrupt. For such reasons it appears justified, in particular, to reduce the required severance payments. In addition, the current rules probably place unrealistically high responsibilities on distressed enterprises to initiate individual adjustment measures during the 6-month notification period before dismissal. In general, experience in Slovenia and elsewhere does not suggest that enterprises which themselves are faced with major restructuring needs are particularly well placed to help their workers find jobs elsewhere. Worse still, if enterprise managers are put under too much moral and financial pressure to assume such responsibilities, there is a risk that their attention will be unduly distracted from their most important task: to restructure their businesses in ways that can generate profits and viable jobs.

Finally, public policies to oversee the wage-setting process may have been justified in the transition years, but the need for continued public intervention of the kinds used at present is questionable. In particular, the government should probably avoid policies which directly or indirectly promote a practice of wage bargaining at several levels. Multi-tier bargaining can make it difficult to establish who is responsible for the final wage outcome. A move towards a bargaining model with fewer tiers may therefore be justified, and should in any case not be blocked by government intervention. In the long run, the efficiency of the wage-setting system will probably depend, above all, on an effective management of enterprises and on the budgetary constraints they face.

3

THE NATIONAL EMPLOYMENT OFFICE
AND ITS PROGRAMMES

INTRODUCTION

Already before the break-up of the Yugoslav federation, Slovenia had a network of public employment service offices, an unemployment compensation system and a few active labour market programmes. The provisions were broadly similar throughout Yugoslavia, but in general the federal authorities did not wield many powers in this policy area. Most of the pertinent legislation had been adopted at republic level, while the financing and implementation was even more decentralised: employer and employee contributions for unemployment insurance and related programmes were collected and spent by "self-managed communities of interest", covering small local districts[29].

Since 1991, the employment service has been reorganised as a national agency, instructed to implement its policies uniformly throughout Slovenia. Under its new name, the *Republiski Zavod za Zaposlovanje*, or the National Employment Office (NEO), has substantially increased its staff and expenditure. The range of its activities has been gradually modified in response to the new social and economic situation, but many institutional characteristics can still be traced to the Yugoslav past.

This chapter analyses the principal elements of these policies as they have been pursued in the past few years, with special focus on some key problems and policy options that may face decision makers in the near future. Above all, it concentrates on policies for unemployed individuals, addressing the question of how well the NEO has responded to the substantial increase in unemployment since the 1980s. As shown, the effectiveness of this policy response has been restrained by the fact that the agency must also accomplish a number of other obligations, which it has inherited from the past.

The chapter first reviews the institutional framework and the size of expenditure for labour market programmes. It then considers the network of employment offices and their functions, the unemployment insurance system, the job-brokering function and the main types of active labour market programmes.

LEGAL AND INSTITUTIONAL FRAMEWORK

The NEO, led by a tripartite administrative council, is a public agency reporting to Slovenia's Ministry of Labour, Family and Social Affairs. The Parliament adopts annual budgets for the NEO on the basis of its work programmes; further budgetary conditions can be specified in contracts between the Ministry and the NEO. These procedures were designed to reserve a degree of formal autonomy for the NEO at the implementation stage, but they have proved rather time-consuming, with disturbing effects on the agency's planning. In 1995, the budget for the year was adopted only in the third quarter, while the 1996 budget was adopted in the second quarter.

Employers and employees pay contributions, altogether 0.2 per cent of the wage sum in 1996, for the nominal purpose of financing unemployment benefits, of which they cover about one-fourth of the expenses. But in practice the government treats these contributions as part of its general revenues, with no earmarking for particular types of spending. This pragmatic approach to financing, paralleled in many OECD and other transition countries, should permit a relatively simple budget administration and a rapid implementation of political decisions. It means, however, that the NEO has no automatically predictable revenues, making it all the more dependent on a timely adoption of its annual budgets.

Most NEO activities have their legal foundation in a 1991 Law on Employment and Unemployment Insurance, which mentions all the main tasks normally associated with a public employment service: job-brokering, vocational guidance, unemployment compensation and active labour market programmes (*e.g.* training and several types of job subsidy). This law, however, was conceived at an early stage of the transition and before Slovenia's independence, and many of its provisions are not so well adapted to the needs of the present labour market, with for example a much larger number of small employers and new forms of temporary employment. A revision of the law is under way.

The NEO's relations with employers have traditionally been marked by its role as a public authority, with legal and administrative powers, rather than as a service provider. Employers are still obliged to notify vacancies and fill them "in co-operation" with the NEO[30], and this is enforced with a strictness that has few counterparts in other countries – albeit, as will be seen, in a perfunctory manner, sometimes involving more paperwork than actual job-brokering.

The NEO has two functions not normally associated with public employment services, namely to issue work permits to foreigners and to administer means-tested scholarships for students. It also devotes considerable efforts to vocational guidance for students in primary and secondary education. The tasks related to scholarships and vocational guidance have become more burdensome as a result of the reduced role of enterprises in the educational area. (As mentioned in

Chapter 1, enterprises were previously more involved, because – in theory if not always in practice – all secondary education courses were designed to lead to particular jobs.) The proportion of youths seeking guidance from the NEO at the end of compulsory schooling has increased, reaching 80 per cent in 1995. The possibility of transferring some or all of these tasks concerning students to schools or other bodies is under consideration, and some progress in this direction has been made with regard to vocational guidance, at least in one region visited by the OECD team of examiners. Under current rules, however, schools cannot be forced to provide vocational guidance, and they do not always have staff with the necessary qualifications.

PRIVATE EMPLOYMENT SERVICES

The NEO has no complete monopoly on brokerage, apart from placements abroad, but private employment agencies must be authorised by the Ministry. Such authorisations are limited to particular labour-market segments: only the NEO can offer general employment services. Fees may be charged only from employers. With these limitations, authorisations are awarded to applicant firms that fulfil certain legal conditions, especially with regard to staff qualifications.

In 1996, 20 private employment agencies were in operation, up from 18 in the preceding year. They achieved about 12 000 placements in 1995, of which 80 per cent concerned temporary jobs without formal employment contracts. The jobs typically required specialised skills, e.g. in language or music teaching, or in accounting and related consultancy services. In other words, the role of private agencies appears insignificant for jobs with longer duration. (It probably concerns well below 1 per cent of all hires, compared with 8 per cent for the NEO, according to the LFS; see below[31].)

In addition, about 80 specialised temporary-work agencies play an important role for students in secondary and higher education, for example with respect to summer jobs. Some of them can also help the students find traineeship jobs at the end of education. About 85 000 students, including most of the 44 000 persons enrolled in the country's two universities, performed temporary work through such agencies during 1996. The popularity of this form of work appears to be explained, in part, by its exemption from most social security contributions (except for work injury and occupational disease).

OVERVIEW IN BUDGETARY TERMS

The Slovenian government's expenditure on labour market programmes was over 2 per cent of GDP in 1992 and 1993, but has fallen subsequently; in 1995 it was 1.4 per cent of GDP (Table 3.1). Almost one-half of the total for 1995 was

Table 3.1. **Public expenditure on labour market programmes as a percentage of GDP**

Programme category	1990	1991	1992	1993	1994	1995	Average in 1994 for	
							OECD[1]	EU and EFTA
1. Public employment services and administration	**0.06**	**0.06**	**0.08**	**0.07**	**0.11**	**0.13**	**0.1**	**0.2**
2. Labour market training	**0.10**	**0.06**	**0.07**	**0.11**	**0.06**	**0.08**	**0.2**	**0.3**
a. Training of unemployed adults ("preparation for employment")	0.03	0.01	0.04	0.07	0.04	0.06		
b. Training of redundant workers	0.07	0.04	0.03	0.04	0.02	0.02		
3. Youth measures (subsidies to employers who hire trainees)	**0.08**	**0.17**	**0.20**	**0.19**	**0.08**	**0.07**	**0.1**	**0.2**
4. Subsidised employment	**0.20**	**0.56**	**0.88**	**0.45**	**0.35**	**0.36**	**0.1**	**0.2**
a. Subsidies to employers	0.02	0.44	0.82	0.36	0.23	0.24		
b. Support of unemployed persons starting enterprises	0.18	0.11	0.03	0.04	0.07	0.08		
c. Direct job creation (community works)	–	0.01	0.03	0.04	0.05	0.04		
5. Measures for the disabled	**0.01**	**0.02**	**0.02**	**0.02**	**0.03**	**0.04**	**0.1**	**0.2**
a. Vocational rehabilitation	0.01	0.01	0.01	0.01	0.01	0.02		
b. Work for the disabled	–	0.01	0.01	0.00	0.02	0.02		
6. Unemployment compensation	**0.26**	**0.57**	**0.82**	**1.22**	**1.13**	**0.75**	**1.0**	**1.8**
7. Early retirement for labour market reasons	**0.17**	**0.26**	**0.14**	**0.03**	**–**	**–**	**0.1**	**0.2**
Total	**0.87**	**1.70**	**2.20**	**2.08**	**1.77**	**1.43**	**1.7**	**3.1**
Active measures (1-5)	0.45	0.87	1.25	0.83	0.64	0.68	0.6	1.1
Passive measures (6-7)	0.43	0.83	0.96	1.25	1.13	0.75	1.1	2.0

– Nil or less than 0.005.
1. Countries that were OECD members in 1993, except Turkey.
Sources: OECD; NEO; Ministry of Labour, Family and Social Affairs.

devoted to active measures (including the cost of running offices), a higher proportion than in most OECD and transition countries. The spending on active measures alone was also relatively high in relation to GDP, compared with the OECD area as a whole and most transition countries, although it was modest compared with Western Europe.

Most expenditure on active measures concern employment subsidies, of which many are administered by the Ministry and not by the NEO. Until 1995, at least, the largest of these subsidy schemes aimed to preserve existing jobs. But the NEO can offer a variety of supports for job hires, self-employment and community work. Training measures have until now been less significant in terms of expenditure, but nevertheless affect many persons. The "passive" group of programmes consists mainly of unemployment benefits, but in the early 1990s the NEO also spent considerable amounts on early retirement (especially the now-abandoned practice of "purchasing" pension rights for displaced workers). More details about the principal programmes are given below.

THE OFFICE NETWORK AND ITS STAFFING

The NEO has 10 regional and 59 local employment offices, organised in a uniform manner. Contacts with job-seekers essentially take place in the local offices, which are managed by regional offices and have almost no administrative functions of their own. Until recently, most local office districts used to correspond to municipalities, but following an increase in the number of municipalities it has become recognised that one office can serve several of them. The size of a local office district is moderate by international standards, on average having about 33 000 inhabitants of whom 2 000 are registered as unemployed and less than 1 000 receive benefits.

Staff numbers are fixed in the NEO's annual contracts with the Ministry. The total has increased constantly since the late 1980s, but still falls short of a planning target of slightly under 1 000. The number was about 800 at the end of 1996, up from 547 three years earlier. About 80 staff members served in the national headquarters, while 350 were in regional offices; local offices also employed about 350 persons, of whom just under 300 were responsible for job information and placement. Relatively large resources are devoted to administrative tasks, including the issuing of work permits to foreigners and scholarships to students, while 120 specialised staff members are engaged in vocational guidance, mostly in schools. For the future, it appears important to find a solution that would enable the NEO to focus more on its core functions.

A local office typically has between 2 and 22 staff members, with an average of 6 – *i.e.* offices are generally small compared with the corresponding averages in most OECD and transition countries (which fall, with few exceptions, in the range of 15 to 50)[32]. The proportion of total staff allocated to local offices is also low by international standards. A reduction of the regional administration could possibly release more staff for client contacts; however, the local offices often depend on practical support from the regional level, because most of them are too small to provide many specialised services themselves. Most regional offices are located together with some of the larger local ones, forming a combined office unit with, typically, 40 to 50 staff members – most of whom, however, have administrative functions or other tasks that involve no contact with the unemployed.

On average, there is about one NEO officer for 150 registered unemployed persons, or one officer for about 50 recipients of unemployment benefits. If this is compared with similar estimates for other countries [OECD, 1995a, 1995b (Table 3), 1996a and 1996c)], the NEO appears moderately understaffed in relation to the unemployed, but quite well staffed in relation to the benefit recipients. Considering, moreover, that less than half of the total NEO staff are engaged in job-brokering, it emerges that the average job-broker must serve 400 to 500 registered unemployed persons, of whom fewer than 150 receive unemployment benefits. The last-mentioned figure, which only takes account of the benefit recipients, suggests a moderate workload by most international standards, one that is close to certain targets for staffing which have occasionally been cited as desirable elsewhere[33]. But in practice, the actual workload per counsellor may be about twice as great, because not all job-brokering staff are in charge of contacts with job-seekers. Moreover, at least some of the numerous job-seekers who do not receive benefits should also be treated with priority. Therefore, an efficient management of the resources for counselling would also seem to require a better system for identifying the principal target groups.

NEO staff are generally well educated, but not always very experienced: about half of them have been in the organisation for under three years. About one-third of the total staff are university-level graduates, while many have shorter post-secondary education, often in the area of social work.

UNEMPLOYMENT BENEFITS

Unemployment compensation comes in two forms: income-related benefits and a means-tested flat-rate unemployment assistance. Both are part of an insurance scheme, compulsory for all employees, with a possibility for the self-employed and some other groups to enrol voluntarily[34]. As a last resort – described in the next chapter – unemployed people may also obtain social assistance from the offices in charge of general welfare (Centres for Social Work).

Less than half of the registered unemployed receive benefits of any kind, largely because the rules about unemployment benefits exclude first-job seekers and many of the long-term unemployed, as explained below. At the end of 1995, only some 34 000 persons received unemployment compensation, including

28 000 cases of income-related and 6 000 cases of means-tested flat-rate benefits. In addition, judging from the LFS in May 1996, social assistance was the only source of income for about 14 000 registered unemployed persons. The total number of workers depending on public income transfers due to unemployment can therefore be estimated at 48 000, or about 40 per cent of the registered unemployed.

Principal conditions

In order to qualify for unemployment benefits, the claimant must have worked and paid insurance contributions without interruption during the last nine months. If the work was not continuous, it must have lasted for 12 out of the last 18 months. Thus, contrary to the situation in some countries, no benefits other than social assistance can be paid to first-job seekers and others with less than nine months of work experience. As an exception, youths who have finished traineeship jobs (internships) can obtain flat-rate benefits even if these jobs did not last nine months. Only formal employment is counted, not subsidised work for the community (see below).

The penalty rules for workers who leave jobs against the will of the employers or are dismissed by their own fault are more strict than in most countries. In general, such behaviour will exclude the worker from benefits for the whole duration of unemployment, and not only for some specified sanction period[35]. This rule may possibly be too strict, in view of the desirability of encouraging a certain volume of labour-market turnover. It could, for example, discourage redundant workers and the unemployed from trying jobs that they are not sure they want.

Income-related benefits correspond to 70 per cent of previous earnings during the first three months of unemployment, thereafter 60 per cent. The calculation is made on the basis of average earnings during the last three months. The maximum benefit is 3.2 times the guaranteed income (a unit determined periodically for social security purposes), *i.e.* 3.2 times 34 107 Tolars per month in the last quarter of 1996. This corresponds to about 85 per cent of the average before-tax wage – a modest ceiling by international standards.

These benefits can be paid for the following maximum periods, depending on the length of time a benefit claimant has been at work and insured:

- 3 months of benefit after 9 months of work if it was continuous, otherwise after 12 months;
- 6 months of benefit after 30 months of work if it was continuous, otherwise after 50 months;
- 9 months of benefit after 5 years of work;
- 12 months of benefit after 10 years of work;
- 8 months of benefit after 15 years of work;
- 24 months of benefit after 20 years of work.

As an exception, persons entitled to a pension within three years from the end of these periods can continue to receive income-related benefits until they retire, if they cannot find a job.

Workers who exhaust their right to income-related benefits are entitled to unemployment assistance, which they can receive for a further six months. The assistance benefit is equal to 80 per cent of the guaranteed income, or about 25 per cent of the average before-tax wage, which is also the minimum amount of the income-related benefits. However, the assistance is not paid if the household income per person exceeds 80 per cent of the guaranteed income.

No unemployment benefits are paid to persons with assets from which they could earn more than the minimum unemployment benefit (as declared by the applicants; some checks are made with the help of public registers). However, since 1993, benefits can be combined with so-called contract work, without a formal employee relationship, paying up to twice the minimum benefit, *i.e.* about one-half of the average wage.

This two-tier benefit system is relatively generous compared with other transition countries, and in some respects it is comparable to those of a number of OECD countries with relatively extensive provisions, *e.g.* France, Germany and the Nordic countries. However, as shown by the above analysis, it is not so generous in two important respects. First, it excludes all cases of self-inflicted unemployment, *i.e.* about 20 000 persons or 15 per cent of those on the register. Secondly, the duration of benefits is not very long unless the claimant has several years of work experience; apart from the oldest group, there is no possibility to obtain benefits indefinitely (as is possible, for example, with unemployment assistance in Germany). Nor can insurance entitlements be renewed by participation in community work (as, for example, in Sweden). As a result, the maximum compensation periods are frequently exhausted. At the end of 1995, as many as 32 000 persons, or 25 per cent of the unemployed, had been on the register for over three years. (As seen in Chapter 1, the incidence of such very long-term registered unemployment is tending to increase, in spite of a fall in unemployment lasting more than one year.) Other groups of registered unemployed persons without benefits numbered about 42 000, including some 27 000 first-job seekers and many with less than nine months of work experience.

Job-search and availability requirements

A basic condition for unemployment benefits, in Slovenia as elsewhere, is that the claimant seeks work and is available for it. Studies of the public employment service in various countries (OECD, 1995*a*, 1995*b*, 1996*a*) have shown that enforcing this condition is a major difficulty in the day-to-day practice of labour market policy. However, a suitable set of controls are especially important when benefits and duration limits are generous – and, conversely, the more effectively the conditions are enforced, the more generous benefit levels and duration limits can be adopted without negative effects on the labour market. In general, enforcement tends to be most strict when job vacancies are numerous compared with unemployment (*e.g.* in the Czech Republic, or in Sweden before the 1990s), while it is often lax in other labour market situations.

Persons registered as unemployed by the NEO, whether claiming benefits or not, must in principle come to the office once a month. This obligation is not consistently applied in all offices, but probably most individuals who claim benefits are called in monthly. These mandatory appointments can sometimes consist of a simple signing-up procedure, handled by administrative staff in the offices. Recently, however, at least two regional offices visited by the OECD examiners have begun to require as a rule about 15 minutes of counselling per month for every benefit claimant. Usually, a client will then meet the same counsellor every time, following an individual job-search plan set up during the first interview, as is also the practice in certain other countries[36]. Further compulsory elements are sometimes used on an experimental basis, such as requiring benefit claimants to supply proof from employers about their job search[37].

In some regions, more lax practices may still prevail, with counselling offered essentially as a voluntary service for clients who ask for it. Where this is the situation, persons who are not interested may never be confronted with the need to discuss their situation with a counsellor.

But a counsellor may always call an unemployed person to the office if there is a suitable job. If a job offer is refused, the worker is liable to lose the benefits for the remaining part of the unemployment spell. The number of such cases is low, however. One office visited by the OECD team did not use job offers for control purposes, while another office did so to some extent[38]. In the country as a whole, there are a few hundred cases per year in which benefit terminations are formally justified by job refusals; possibly, there are more cases which *de facto* involve such a sanction without being recorded as such[39].

The law specifies that a job is "suitable", in the sense that a benefit claimant cannot refuse it, if it corresponds to the claimant's education and capability[40]. If the last job was one or two educational steps lower, according to Slovenia's classification of types of education, a similar job must be accepted again. Temporary jobs are generally regarded as suitable. Half-time jobs must also be accepted (although they are not very common, as seen in Chapter 1), but they may be combined with receipt of partial unemployment benefits if the previous job was full-time.

JOB-BROKERING

Main features

The basic job information and brokerage functions were not so important before the economic transition. At that time, the allocation of workers to jobs was influenced by many administrative procedures in enterprises, schools and related public bodies, but the idea of job-brokering as a mediation between actors in a market only gained ground slowly in the 1980s. A modernisation of the employment service was then initiated, however, and the vacancy information system was computerised by 1990. After becoming independent, Slovenia expanded the job-brokering activity and changed it in various ways in response to the new situation. But this process is far from complete. Indeed, in Slovenia as in OECD countries, this vital task will justify a sustained policy emphasis on research and development and critical assessment of the results achieved.

The NEO's job-brokering relies to a great extent on self-service facilities, including weekly advertisements in newspapers and the use of Teletext and an Internet home page. Individualised counselling is sometimes – although to a varying extent, as seen above – provided as regular interviews with benefit claimants. In addition, it is offered on a voluntary basis to those who ask for it, within the often narrow constraints of available staff time. Some priority is given to the long-term unemployed (over one year), the elderly, those without vocational qualifications, first-job seekers and the disabled.

To permit more effective monitoring of individuals, it appears especially important at present – in Slovenia as in many countries (OECD, 1996a) – to extend as far as possible the practice of calling job seekers for counselling at regular intervals. It would probably be justified to increase both the duration of the compulsory interviews and the numbers of persons they concern. A problem, which appears inevitable, is that this is likely to reduce the amount of staff time available to the more motivated clients who ask for counselling at their own initiative. However, considering that the NEO is also responsible for preventing abuse of unemployment benefits, its counsellors must combine a control function with their more client-friendly service role[41].

Another key problem, affecting the job-brokering by any method, is that the NEO's two large information systems – for vacancies and job-seekers – are not entirely well suited to a market-oriented service function. Reminiscent of the previous administrative approach to labour market policy, they produce much "official" information to comply with the law – covering virtually all recruitment decisions by enterprises – instead of focusing on the information most likely to be useful to job-seekers and employers. For example, worker qualifications are recorded according to formal education, but not work experience. However, these information systems are also characterised by a high degree of transparency, which can be regarded as an advantage.

The policy issues at stake here fall under three sub-headings. The first two concern vacancies and job-seekers, while the third is devoted to Job Clubs and related activities.

Vacancies

Based on mandatory notifications by employers, the NEO's vacancy lists cover virtually all job openings that exist in the "formal" employment sector, but not necessarily those in non-standard types of employment. Within the formal sector, the mandatory notification system is enforced to a larger extent than in any OECD country. This is achieved with the help of the health insurance administration: in order to become insured, any newly hired person must provide a certificate from the NEO showing that the job had first been listed as vacant. [Similarly strict rules, amounting in effect to a compulsory notification of hires rather than vacancies, were applied until recently in Italy and Spain. Other countries with experience of compulsory vacancy listing – e.g. the Czech Republic and Sweden – have generally not found it practicable to enforce (OECD, 1993, 1995a and 1996a).]

The resulting vacancy statistics are exaggerated because they include jobs for which the employers already have candidates. In the previous economic system, this seems to have served to promote transparency and some amount of co-ordination with regard to employers' hiring practices; however, such information is not very relevant to the NEO's present tasks. It appears that many employers comply perfunctorily with the law by simply delaying their formal hiring decisions until after a stipulated deadline for applications (usually eight days)[42]. Such "false" vacancies are not legally distinguishable from "real" ones, and are therefore included in official vacancy statistics. However, when employers notify vacancies, they are asked to specify whether they want assistance in finding candidates; in 1995, they made such declarations in only 32 per cent of the cases[43]. The cases when employers wanted the NEO's help seem to have concerned mostly low-skill jobs, especially in the non-commercial sector.

The total inflow of vacancies – "real" or "false" – has more than doubled in the 1990s, surpassing 150 000 per year in 1994 and 1995. The number of "real" vacancies per year may therefore have been in the order of 50 000, corresponding to about 7 per cent of Slovenia's dependent labour force. (By comparison, some of the best-resourced employment service agencies in OECD countries received vacancy inflows corresponding to 10 to 15 per cent of the dependent labour force in 1994[44].) As in most countries, a high proportion of the vacancies – 60 per cent in total during 1995, somewhat less for "real" vacancies – concern temporary jobs, lasting on average six months.

Local offices display the vacancy information on notice boards and in printed lists, the latter being updated twice a week. In addition, the whole vacancy database for Slovenia is regularly published in major newspapers, and it is available to the general public for interactive job search via electronic media (Teletext and the Internet). All vacancies are then presented in a standard format, indicating whether the employers have expressed interest in receiving applications. Employers' names and addresses are mentioned, so that individuals can contact them without asking NEO staff.

Offices visited by the OECD examiners had notice boards outside the buildings, so that they could be consulted when the offices were closed. Further self-service material was available in the reception halls. Only administrative staff were present in these halls: clients in need of personal advice had to ask for appointments with counsellors.

The somewhat bureaucratic character of the vacancy listing is underlined by the practice of displaying each job notice until a stipulated application deadline, which must precede the employer's formal decision to hire someone. Most vacancies are then withdrawn automatically, regardless of whether they have been filled or not. This contrasts with the practice in most OECD countries, where vacancies are normally displayed until they are filled or withdrawn by the employers. The difference explains why Slovenia's vacancy statistics are expressed only in flow terms: stock data would not add much information. (In most OECD countries, by contrast, stock data about unfilled vacancies can be useful as indicators of labour shortage.)

The possibility of making vacancy notifications voluntary for employers is currently being considered. Such a reform would relieve the NEO of much paperwork and enable it to devote more attention to "real" vacancies. It would also put more pressure on the offices to improve their services to employers, so as to make it worthwhile for them to continue notifying their vacancies.

Until now, few NEO staff have been specialised in helping employers. On-site visits suggested that many job-brokering counsellors never visit enterprises, although they may have telephone contacts with them. One possible way to improve this situation, tried in some regions, involves the creation of small specialised offices for employers – a solution which, however, does not exclude that the staff of the other offices may also need to develop their employer contacts. It may also be justified to give employers who notify vacancies a wider choice among different types of intervention, ranging from the mere publication of their vacancies to an individualised assistance in selecting candidates.

If employers are given a choice, some of them might prefer procedures in which their names are not revealed until the NEO has preselected some candidates for the vacancies. Previous OECD studies have shown that an "open" treatment of vacancy information – *i.e.* with publication of employers' names, as in Slovenia – is generally favoured in countries with moderate unemployment (*e.g.* Austria, the Czech Republic, Japan and Norway), while employers elsewhere have sometimes resisted such openness for fear of receiving too many applicants. This risk, however, can also be reduced by more precise specifications of the job requirements, something that several countries have found essential in any case. Provided that the quality and relevance of the vacancy information can be assured, the potential advantages of self-service and new media for electronic communication are probably greatest with an open procedure. Perhaps, the best policy would be to let employers decide, while still recommending openness as the method preferred by the employment service.

Job-seekers

The NEO's registration of job-seekers is intended, according to the law, to cover both the unemployed and workers who want to change jobs. These two groups are in principle to be distinguished from each other, but – as already seen – the NEO cannot be said to have accomplished the task of identifying the persons who are really unemployed. As a further complication, the legal definition of unemployment excludes not only the employed, but also all persons having assets from which they could earn a living equivalent to the guaranteed income. In practice, almost all of the about 120 000 persons on register in 1996 were treated as unemployed, while a separate list contained some 1 200 job-seekers with assets. A further 10 000 to 15 000 employed job-seekers seemed to be merely taken note of by individual counsellors, and not formally registered[45]. As an experimental initiative, used on a small scale, job-seekers can also present their *curriculum vitae* on one of the NEO's Internet pages, so that they can be studied on line by potential employers.

Until recently, very few job-seekers were ever de-registered against their wishes, although the law requires such a step in certain situations. Those who have twice refused suitable jobs or missed appointments with the NEO are liable to be removed from the register (cf. the sanctions mentioned above for unemployment benefit claimants, who can lose their benefits after only one job refusal). After such a sanction, the person concerned can be registered again after six months.

Following a new set of procedural rules introduced in 1995, the NEO has sent questionnaires to large numbers of registered persons, asking them to confirm their willingness to accept work or training, and made other checks with the help of the population register. This led to de-registration in many individual cases, but the overall impact on registered unemployment was small, partly because the principles for registration of new clients were not changed at the same time. Further special efforts of this nature are planned, perhaps as a recurrent activity.

More fundamentally, the quality of information in the register depends to a large extent on the nature of counselling and other regular contacts between the NEO and its clients. In this operational context, it is generally unfortunate if the register is treated too much as an end in itself (with a view to legal or statistical implications), rather than simply as a list of persons requiring NEO attention, classified according to the nature of the services they need.

A dilemma here, apparently, is that the NEO lacks resources to interview all job-seekers regularly, while it also – partly as a result of this – has too little systematic information about individuals to know which persons it would be justified to interview more often. In this situation, as indicated, counsellors concentrate mostly on benefit recipients; in addition, according to the government's instructions, they must pay special attention to first-job seekers and the long-term unemployed, who typically receive no benefits. These instructions do not solve the targeting problem, because the three groups just mentioned make up three-fourths or more of registered unemployment.

New approaches to job counselling

For the future, new procedures are under discussion in which every new client, and not only the benefit claimants, would be called at least once to a substantive interview with a qualified counsellor. This would serve to identify more individual problems immediately, and to establish a plan for job-search and further measures. The usefulness of a system with compulsory new-client interviews has been demonstrated in evaluations, notably in Canada and the United Kingdom[46]. However, at least initially – judging from on-site visits – this procedure will mainly concern those who claim unemployment benefits.

In this context it is also intended, at least in some regions (such as Kranj, visited by the OECD examiners), to assign one counsellor as a personal contact for every newly registered person. This counsellor would then be responsible for setting up the individual job-search plan. As a voluntary complement, job-seekers will also be offered the opportunity to participate in a two-day workshop about job search, designed to encourage a quick return to work.

In 1995, the NEO began to organise Job Clubs, following the example of other European countries. These clubs offer intensified job-search training and practical assistance, principally for those with over six months of unemployment, but also for first-job seekers. Job Clubs last three weeks, but participants can come back during a three-month period. In addition, regional offices sometimes organise workshops in matters of social adjustment for the long-term unemployed. Participation in all these activities is voluntary.

Effects on job finding

Slovenia does not produce statistics about placements, as this term is defined in most countries, *i.e.* job referrals leading to employment. The NEO counts the vacancies officially reported as filled, about 90 000 in 1995; but this includes all hires of registered job-seekers approved for health insurance – subject to the condition, as described above, that the employers must first have notified the jobs as vacant. In other words, it tallies with a certain administrative involvement of the public authorities in enterprises' recruitment activity, but does not assume any active job-brokering.

The cited number of filled vacancies corresponds to only 58 per cent of the notified vacancies ("real" or not), the remainder never being reported as filled. Such a low vacancy-filling rate could reflect a problem of labour shortage; however, some of the officially unfilled vacancies – not least for temporary jobs – may in fact have been filled, but never reported as such for the purpose of health insurance.

In the absence of relevant administrative statistics, the job-finding effect of employment services may be studied through surveys of workers or employers. The LFS, which asks employed respondents how they found their jobs, suggests a falling market share. Among those who entered dependent employment in the past few years (excluding mobility within firms), the proportion citing the NEO as the main source of information fell from 13 per cent in 1993 to 8 per cent in 1996. Similar survey-based market share estimates in OECD countries have often been of the same order of magnitude (OECD, 1996e, Chapter 4).

EMPLOYMENT AND TRAINING PROGRAMMES

Slovenia's labour market policies include several types of enterprise subsidy, of which the largest part – each year concerning firms with over 50 000 employees – is administered at central Ministry level (Table 3.2). During the early 1990s, such measures were largely a matter of discretionary government decision, but since 1994 they have followed publicised criteria, with fixed application procedures involving a special Ministry commission.

The NEO's active labour market programmes have a greater element of individual targeting, compared with those of the Ministry, focusing especially on the unemployed but also on redundant employees. While quantitatively modest, these programmes include the main options usually found in OECD and other transition countries: training in enterprises or classroom courses; subsidies towards hiring in ordinary jobs, self-employment or community work; special measures for people with disabilities. Most of these schemes give priority to long-term unemployed persons (over one year), and often also to first-job seekers, especially when they have no qualification above the level of primary education.

In 1995, the NEO placed about 40 000 of its clients in active programmes (not counting those of the Ministry), for an average period of four months. About 15 000 of these persons entered subsidised jobs or traineeships, implying that the NEO subsidised about one-sixth of all hires recorded as flows out of the unemployment register; a further 3 000 started self-employment and roughly 20 000 were placed in the NEO's training or vocational rehabilitation schemes. The following sub-sections give more detail about each programme.

Table 3.2. **Participants in active labour market programmes**

Programme or programme category (numbered as in Table 3.1)	Programme entries per year						Stock number of participants in June				
	1991	1992	1993	1994	1995	1996 (planned)	1991	1992	1993	1994	1995
2. Labour market training	**19 082**	**18 291**	**30 684**	**19 431**	**27 235**	..	..	..	..	**4 014**	**4 011**
a. Training of unemployed adults ("preparation for employment")	12 000	9 900	17 963	10 768	16 456	..	..	..	..	2 624	2 886
b. Training of redundant workers	7 082	8 391	12 721	8 663	10 779	..	3 541	4 196	5 143	1 390	1 125
Compensation from the NEO during redundancy	7 082	8 391	10 285	2 780	2 250	..	3 541	4 196	5 143	1 390	1 125
Other schemes[1]	–	–	2 436	5 883	8 529	17 400	..	..	..	..	..
3. Youth measures (subsidies to employers who hire trainees)	**7 200**	**9 300**	**13 117**	**8 423**	**5 011**	..	..	..	..	**2 807**	**4 735**
4. Subsidised employment	**6 387**	**15 708**	**45 347**	**77 236**	**65 934**	**50 750**	..	..	..	..	**4 772**
a. Subsidies to employers	3 308	9 822	37 486	69 045	58 451	38 100	..	..	..	580	1 704
Subsidies to preserve productive jobs[1]	..	..	28 199	47 986	43 794	23 300	..	..	..	..	..
Redundancies in state-owned firms[1]	..	..	7 939	14 101	6 659	1 500	..	..	..	..	..
Support of hires in new productive jobs[1]	3 308	9 822	1 348	5 693	4 754	11 500	..	..	..	..	..
Hiring subsidy for first-job seekers, long-term unemployed, UB recipients (refunding of social security contrib.)	–	2 373	–	1 265	3 244	1 800	..	..	..	580	1 704
b. Support of unemployed persons starting enterprises	1 831	2 373	3 494	3 716	3 211	2 250	..	..	..	332	345
c. Direct job creation (community works)	1 248	3 513	4 367	4 475	4 272	10 400	..	..	..	2 308	2 723
5. Measures for people with disabilities	**362**	**424**	**852**	**4 993**	**6 309**	**4 415**	–	**664**	**619**	**2 649**	**3 460**
a. Vocational rehabilitation (training and medical service)[2]	362	424	732	2 337	3 028	4 185	..	..	..	669	507
b. Work for the disabled	..	..	120	2 656	3 281	230	..	664	619	1 980	2 953
TOTAL	**33 031**	**43 723**	**90 000**	**110 083**	**104 489**	..	..	..	..	..	**16 978**

.. Data not available.
– Nil or less than half of the last digit used.
1. Administered by the Ministry of Labour, Family and Social Affairs.
2. The stock data only cover training.
Sources: NEO (1996); Ministry of Labour, Family and Social Affairs.

Job subsidies

Subsidies to ordinary employers

In 1994 and 1995, the dominant subsidy programme managed by the Ministry of Labour, Family and Social Affairs aimed to preserve productive jobs. In each of the two years, about 3 billion Tolars were paid to between 200 and 300 enterprises which together provided over 40 000 jobs. This programme gives priority to labour-intensive industries that are net exporters, e.g. the clothing, shoe and timber industries. Applicant firms must be engaged in restructuring and have a chance of becoming viable, while not yet meeting the requirements of the new market situation. A substantial reduction of this programme was foreseen in the budget for 1996[47].

Another programme under the Ministry of Labour, Family and Social Affairs covers part of the redundancy costs in state-owned enterprises and forestry. This includes firms that are wholly owned by the Development Fund, often because they have been difficult to privatise[48]. The Ministry contributes to the wage costs during the six-month notice period which is mandatory before dismissal for economic reasons. (During this period, as explained in Chapter 2, redundant workers' wages are usually reduced by 30 per cent if they do not work or undergo training, although they must not be lower than the minimum wage.) The spending in 1995 was about 800 million Tolars and concerned 6 600 workers.

Other employers cannot receive public support for redundancy costs in general. However, if they organise training or other adjustment measures for redundant workers, both the Ministry and the NEO have some funds to support it. Until 1993, these measures also included the "purchase" of pension rights, but this practice has been abandoned.

The Ministry also supports the creation of new productive jobs in which registered unemployed persons are hired. This support can consist of a grant for each job, and an interest-rate subsidy if the employer takes a bank loan. In 1995, about 800 million Tolars were paid for about 5 000 jobs.

Since 1994, the NEO can support employers who hire workers belonging to one of three target groups: those who have been unemployed for over two years, first-job seekers and unemployment benefit recipients. This subsidy, consisting of reimbursement of employers' social security contributions for six months, concerned about 2 000 hires in 1995.

Finally, the NEO subsidises traineeships (also called internships), a form of work experience for young people after secondary education. They previously served as a complement to the "guided" education system (see Box 1 in Chapter 1), and remain one of the principal ports of entry into working life, affecting over 10 000 youths annually. About 30 per cent of all trainees tend to obtain permanent jobs with the same employers at the end of their traineeships. Until 1993, the NEO paid wage subsidies in most of the cases, but in this respect the policy has become more restrictive; about half of the trainees were supported in 1995, mainly including those who had been registered as unemployed for over a year.

Subsidies to unemployed workers starting enterprises

For most of the 1990s, about 3 000 unemployed workers annually have started businesses of their own with NEO support. In such cases the unemployed can receive their unemployment benefits as a lump sum, or a grant if they are not entitled to such benefits. The NEO also offers counselling and training seminars in matters of business management, a type of service that has been gradually extended and is currently used by most of the persons concerned. In effect, in Slovenia as in many countries, the employment service is the principal channel for public support of enterprise start-ups: no other state agency has specialised competence or funds for such purposes. However, such activities must largely be contracted out, because they essentially fall outside the range of skills held by NEO staff.

Community work and sheltered workshops

About 3 000 workers on average are employed in community work, mostly organised by local governments with NEO support. They are a matter for annual programming based on publicly advertised invitations to potential organisers, a procedure led by a special Public Works Committee under the NEO's administrative council, representing several ministries and the Slovenian Chamber of Crafts. The jobs are temporary and target the long-term unemployed, who may stay for a year or longer, although the average duration in 1995 was eight months. Participation in community work does not renew unemployment insurance entitlements. Workers receive 70 per cent of the normal wage for equivalent work, to which the NEO contributes 80 per cent of the guaranteed income; the NEO also pays travel costs, lunches and medical care. The workers must continue to seek unsubsidised jobs, and usually receive some counselling and other support, *e.g.* a few days of job-search training. Most participants return to unemployment or leave the labour force afterwards, although in 1995 about 11 per cent of them became permanently employed, often in the social-service sector.

Special permanent jobs for people with disabilities, also numbering about 3 000, are available in 100 sheltered workshops. Many of them were established in the 1990s. The NEO pays grants corresponding to 30 to 70 per cent of the guaranteed income, depending on the degree of disability.

There is also a disability insurance, which, apart from paying pensions (see Chapter 4), can support disabled workers in jobs with ordinary employers, for example by compensating them for reduced wages or working hours. Such allow-

Table 3.3. **Training options financed by the NEO**

	Number of participants				NEO spending per participant entry (expressed as numbers of average monthly wages)[1]	
	Entries		Average stock			
	1994	1995	1994	1995	1994	1995
Basic preparation and social rehabilitation[2]	5 550	10 290	463	858	0.5	0.5
Qualification courses	1 312	2 224	1 968	3 336	1.3	1.3
On the job training:						
– in connection with recruitment	2 555	2 753	639	688	2.4	3.3
– without employment	315	283	79	71	1.3	1.2
Preparation for entry into secondary education[3]	1 036	906	518	453	2.7	2.8
Total	10 768	16 456	3 666	5 406	1.3	1.2

1. The spending per participant entry was divided by the average monthly wage.
2. So-called functional courses.
3. So-called USO courses.
Sources: Annual reports and special submissions from the NEO.

ances are probably paid to most of the approximately 28 000 employed persons classified as disabled.

Training

A programme called "preparation for employment", targeting the NEO's unemployed clients, enrolled about 11 000 persons in 1994 and 16 000 persons in 1995 (Table 3.3). More than one-half of them participated in short "functional" courses, lasting about one month, consisting mainly of basic preparations such as social rehabilitation and literacy teaching, coupled with career planning and job-search assistance. Such courses, which do not involve very high expenditure, appear to serve as a useful complement to the NEO's limited resources for coun-selling of hard-to-place persons.

Vocational training, by contrast, plays a very modest role for unemployed adults by international standards. (In most OECD countries, this is the most impor-tant type of active labour market programme.) In Slovenia, the principal option available consists of on-the-job training, which the NEO may subsidise if a worker has been unemployed for six months. Employers then receive a subsidy about as great as the wage cost during three months, on condition that they hire the persons they train; otherwise the subsidy is lower. About 3 000 workers per year are con-cerned, and most of them are hired by the firms that organise the training. Apparently, any substantial increase of enrolment would be difficult to achieve unless it is accepted that a higher proportion of participants will not obtain any such promise of becoming employed. (In most other countries, training schemes for unemployed people are not normally associated with any hiring commitments.)

Other training and education options mainly target first-job seekers. Most often, the NEO pays for tuition and travel – but not subsistence costs – when youths attend the last grade in secondary vocational education. Such support is available, in principle, for up to one and a half year for persons who have been unemployed for six months. Apparently, this is one of the institutional factors which can make it attractive to register as unemployed for some persons who do not seek work.

Job-seekers with more serious educational shortcomings may participate in so-called USO courses, lasting up to six months and offering basic preparation for entry into secondary education. In this case, which concerns about 1 000 persons per year, the NEO also pays a subsistence allowance.

CONCLUSIONS

A major weakness of the present NEO organisation is that it cannot adequately monitor and support the job-search activity of its unemployed clients. To achieve this objective, it would seem to be necessary, first, to strengthen the efforts already being made to weed out irrelevant individual cases from the client registers. This could probably bring the registered unemployment figure (about 118 000) down to a level similar to that of the LFS unemployment, currently about 70 000, mainly including recipients of unemployment benefits or social assistance, with the addition of the most active job-seekers among the many who are now registered as first-job seekers or in other categories not eligible for benefits (or no longer eligible).

Secondly, it appears crucial that the NEO give sufficient priority to its contacts with individual job-seekers, which should generally be handled by qualified counselling and placement staff. All benefit recipients should be faced with a well-balanced mix of positive job-search assistance, controls and sanctions (*i.e.* both "carrots" and "sticks"). In this respect, some lessons about possible "best-practice" approaches can be drawn from the OECD's international comparisons of the public employment service – although, as is evident from these comparisons, no country can be said to have found the ideal solution (*e.g.* OECD, 1996*a*, 1996*b* and 1996*e*). Above all, it can be concluded that such policy objectives are unlikely to be achieved unless every unemployed person is normally called in for counselling at least once a month.

Assuming that the average job counsellor or placement officer can conduct five interviews per day – each lasting 30 to 40 minutes, implying perhaps an hour's work per interview with preparations – he or she can probably handle a caseload of about 100 to 120 unemployed persons every month, with some time left for other activities such as contacts with employers. On this basis, it would seem that a desirable service level for the about 35 000 unemployment benefit recipients alone would require the NEO to allocate about 400 counsellors entirely to such functions. Furthermore, if some groups among the many who do not receive benefits were to be treated in a similar manner, the staff requirements would be correspondingly higher.

While not entirely unrealistic, such a policy objective would highlight the need for the NEO to streamline its activities, placing a stronger focus on these core tasks. The delivery of scholarships and vocational guidance to students could perhaps be better performed by schools, as is common in several other countries. Moreover, some staff can probably be transferred from regional to local offices, and various administrative routines could be given less emphasis. The registration of job-seekers and vacancies should not be treated as goals in themselves, but only as instruments which the NEO can design and use as convenient in support of its clients.

The notification of vacancies should be voluntary. As in many other countries, the employment service needs to improve its services to employers, who should be given some choice between different types of NEO intervention to fill their vacancies. Employers should also be encouraged to give more details of relevance for placement in their vacancy notices. That said, the present vacancy register system has some distinct advantages, related to its high degree of transparency which makes it suitable for presentation in newspapers and through electronic mass media.

Finally, the NEO's training programmes for unemployed clients are rather small, especially if one considers that most of them actually concern youths, who, perhaps, should be taken care of by the regular education system. The need for NEO support of youths who have not finished their initial education is questionable, and may be even more so in the future, with secondary education offering a wider choice of dual (apprenticeship) programmes as an alternative to the ordinary secondary education. On the other hand, a greater NEO effort in favour of adult vocational training is probably desirable, not least in view of its potential to prevent an excessive use of early retirement. An infrastructure for adult education is largely in place, in the form of secondary and higher education institutions now mainly serving young people, which may be able to cater for more adults in the future.

SOCIAL POLICIES AFFECTING
THE LABOUR MARKET

A growing number of unemployed people – about 15 000 in any month in 1996 – receive social assistance of the general welfare type as their main source of income. This especially concerns youths and long-term unemployed persons who have exhausted their rights to unemployment benefits. However, as shown above in Table 1.7, the numbers of registered unemployed persons in these two groups is substantially larger than 15 000, suggesting that many individuals who may be potentially eligible for social assistance do not apply for it.

Another set of social policy instruments of relevance in a labour market perspective are early retirement and disability pensions. Their use increased substantially in the initial transition years; a decline has since occurred, but the average age of persons entering old-age or disability retirement remains as low as 52 years (see below). All these policies are under the responsibility of the Ministry of Labour, Family and Social Affairs.

Other social policy instruments fall outside the scope of this report. It may be noted, however, that the social insurance system has been retained with small modifications since the 1980s. The number of working days lost in connection with sickness, maternity and work injuries has been relatively stable, apart from a brief peak in the crisis year of 1990. One detail of some relevance to the NEO, as noted in Chapter 1, has to do with the rules about individual health insurance contributions, and notably the fact that municipalities may subsidise these for those who are registered as unemployed. Insofar as this can give unjustified incentives to register at the NEO, the rules should perhaps be modified. In any case, as shown above, NEO registration alone provides no reliable evidence about a person's actual situation.

The chapter first discusses social assistance for unemployed persons, thereafter early retirement and related provisions. In general, the analysis is limited to a labour market policy perspective, with the main focus placed on issues such as work incentives and the opportunity cost of not working for those of working age.

SOCIAL ASSISTANCE

Social assistance benefits are paid by the State and administered by 62 Centres for Social Work, whose districts correspond largely but not entirely to those of the local NEO offices. These centres also provide other services, partly financed by municipalities, which will not be considered here. The pertinent regulations, in a 1992 Law on Social Assistance, have essentially been taken over from before the transition.

In 1995, on average 26 500 persons received social assistance benefits, up from less than 10 000 in 1992 (Table 4.1). Spending increased more, from 0.02 to 0.23 per cent of GDP. The main type of assistance, received by 25 000 persons on average in 1995[49], is called "supplementary benefit" and covers the difference between a household's other incomes and a certain percentage (see below) of the guaranteed income, which was 37 000 Tolars in autumn 1996[50]. Over 60 per cent of those concerned in the second half of 1995 had no other income.

The principal condition for social assistance is that the lack of sufficient income is due to factors "beyond the control" of the applicant. About one-half of the recipients are registered as unemployed at the NEO but receive no unemployment benefits (Table 4.2). Youths aged 18 to 26 are the largest group, corresponding probably to about 40 per cent of the recipients in the second half of 1995. The majority of all recipients were unmarried. About 9 per cent have jobs and receive assistance as a complement to their wages – a situation which thus concerns 0.3 per cent of all employed persons.

The supplementary benefit is up to 52 per cent of the guaranteed income for each adult in a household, plus between 29 and 42 per cent for each child, depending on its age. Youths who have finished their schooling are usually considered as independent, and may therefore receive benefits at the 52 per cent rate, even if they live with their parents. Additional allowances are paid for housing in some cases, and occasionally for one-time expenses. The calculation of family income takes account of most taxable and non-taxable revenues, including unemployment benefits; but exception is made for child allowances up to a limit (22 per cent of the guaranteed income), scholarships, and certain types of assistance to disabled people. Assets are considered only if they can contribute to the household's income.

Table 4.1. **Social assistance benefits**

Average number of recipients

	1985	1990	1992	1993	1994	1995*
Supplementary benefits	7 918	5 100	6 681	15 774	20 914	24 908
Other[1]	2 791	1 893	1 785	1 770	1 709	1 588
Total	10 709	6 993	8 466	17 544	22 623	26 496
Expenditure as a percentage of GDP	n.a.	n.a.	0.02	0.15	0.18	0.23

n.a.: Not available.
* The figures for 1995 are provisional.
1. Mainly for disabled and elderly persons.
Sources: Statistical Yearbook (1995); OECD (1996b); Ministry of Labour, Family and Social Affairs.

Table 4.2.   **Recipients of social assistance as supplementary benefits
by labour-force status**

Percentage distribution in the second half of 1995

Employed	**8.7**
Employees	7.0
Farmers	1.6
Craftsmen	0.1
Potentially job-ready	**63.3**
Registered as unemployed without unemployment benefits	48.5
Persons in need of a supplement to unemployment benefits	3.5
Others	11.2
Not job-ready	**28.0**
Housewives	5.7
Unable to work	5.1
Pensioners	1.8
Students	0.3
Others	15.2
Total	**100**

Note: The cited proportion, derived from administrative data, may be biased by variations in the average length of benefit periods for different groups.
Source: Ministry of Labour, Family and Social Affairs.

In effect, the benefits are usually much lower than the minimum wage (53 500 Tolars), an amount which can only be attained by relatively large families with no other income. In 1995, the average monthly benefit was about 16 750 Tolars, *i.e.* just over 50 per cent of the guaranteed income, but less than 15 per cent of the average wage. To this was added, in about one-tenth of the cases, a rent subsidy of 3 230 Tolars on average.

Decisions to pay assistance can cover a maximum period of six months, which may be renewed. To obtain continuous benefit payments, a client must therefore come to the Centre for Social Work at least twice a year. In the second half of 1995, the average benefit award period was four months, while the maximum period was applied in 40 per cent of the cases (MOLFSA, 1996). In principle, beneficiaries must also notify any change in their financial situation within 15 days, but here the enforcement appears to be lax (Vodopivec, 1996*b*).

Persons who are ready to work must in principle seek jobs, but this is not strictly enforced. The Centres for Social Work usually require them to register at the NEO; occasionally, they may also require participation in community works, rehabilitation or other NEO programmes. However, once the benefits have been awarded for a given period, the centres seldom take many steps to monitor the compliance with such benefit conditions. The NEO, for its part, has no particular procedures for tracking social assistance clients. It usually calls them in once every three months, as is the practice with respect to most unemployed persons who do not receive unemployment benefits. This may be only a formal procedure, without any meeting with a counsellor.

However, as observed in Chapter 3 with regard to the unemployment benefit administration, public income transfers to unemployed persons cannot be effectively managed without regular counselling interviews and a suitable set of controls to enforce the job-search requirement. Assuming, as in Chapter 3, that every unemployed client should ideally be called in for about 30 minutes of counselling once a month, the average counsellor's caseload cannot exceed about 100 to 150 such persons. With currently about 15 000 unemployed social-assistance recipients, it would seem that the NEO would need to devote at least 100 counsellors to these people alone.

But this may be an unrealistic objective for the NEO in the near future, given that this agency must first of all increase its monitoring of clients in receipt of unemployment benefits and unemployment assistance. Against this background, it may be appropriate for the Centres for Social Work to investigate the possibilities to devote more qualified staff of their own to such tasks. This may need to involve, as an average target, about two counsellors per local centre. In any case, there would seem to be a need to strengthen the co-operation between Centres for Social Work and NEO offices.

EARLY RETIREMENT AND DISABILITY PENSIONS

Overview

The median retirement age in Slovenia is low: about 53 years for women and 57.5 years for men in 1995, excluding disability pensioners. The corresponding medians for disability pensioners are nine years lower, suggesting that the overall average for both genders may be in the order of 52 years, down from 56 years in the late 1980s[51]. This fact stands in contrast to the high labour force participation rates recorded for men and women up to about the age of 50 (Table 1.3). It is associated with the provisions of a pension system which in its essentials has been taken over from Yugoslavia, with certain changes adopted in 1992. These changes, as explained below, include a gradual raising of the statutory retirement ages for several groups of persons, to be completed by 1998.

The two years 1990 and 1991 saw an exceptional wave of retirements, involving altogether nearly 80 000 newly pensioned persons, compared with the less than 45 000 that could have been expected from demographic projections. (Each annual cohort in the ages from 50 to 60 included about 22 500 persons.)

Thereafter, in 1993 to 1995, only between 11 000 and 14 000 persons per year have retired, including all types of old-age and disability pension (Tables 4.3 and 4.4). Evidently, these low figures were due in part to the fact that many members of the relevant age groups had retired already in 1990 and 1991; but, in addition, they were influenced by the government's policy to raise the standard retirement ages.

Special early retirement schemes, justified by labour market criteria, have played a role. By and large, however, the situation may also be described as a near-universal tendency for working people to retire before the age of 60, using varying institutional solutions. Three different features of the pension system seem to explain this overall effect.

First, as in many OECD and other transition countries, a substantial proportion of the elderly population retire with disability pensions. These have accounted for

Table 4.3. **Retirements with old-age and disability pensions**

Numbers of new pensioners per year

Type of retirement	1989	1990	1991	1992	1993	1994	1995
Ordinary (old-age)	14 200	22 100	20 600	11 000	4 600	4 900	n.a.
Early retirement for labour market reasons	4 000	9 800	11 400	6 700	3 500	2 300	n.a.
– of which with NEO support ("purchase" of additional rights)	–	–	6 600	4 600	2 100	–	–
Disability	6 000	6 000	8 600	6 500	5 600	4 300	4 000
Total	**24 200**	**37 900**	**40 600**	**24 200**	**13 700**	**11 500**	**11 500**
Memorandum item: Size of an annual population cohort aged 55 or more	22 200	22 200	22 200	22 300	22 400	22 800	n.a.

n.a.:   Not available.
Note: The numbers of early retirements in 1994 and the cohort size before 1993 have been estimated. Survivor pensions are not counted.
Sources: NEO (1996); *Statistical Yearbook* (1994); Vodopivec (1996*a*).

Table 4.4. **Persons receiving pensions**
Average stock numbers

Type of pension	1985	1990	1991	1992	1993	1994	1995
Old-age pensions incl. early retirement	137 000	197 000	231 000	253 000	260 000	262 000	264 000
Disability pensions	68 000	82 000	88 000	92 000	95 000	96 000	97 000
Survivor pensions	70 000	77 000	80 000	81 000	82 000	83 000	84 000
Total excl. survivors	**205 000**	**279 000**	**319 000**	**345 000**	**355 000**	**358 000**	**361 000**

Source: *Statistical Yearbook* (1996).

about one-third of the total flow of persons into retirement in the past few years, up from one-fourth in the late 1980s. (The relative role of disability pensions was lower during the exceptional years 1990 and 1991.)

Secondly, the highest statutory retirement ages, 60 for women and 65 for men, are relevant only to a minority, consisting of healthy persons with between 15 and 20 years of service who are neither long-term unemployed nor have been dismissed from their jobs.

Thirdly, the counting of years of service can often be manipulated. A peculiar provision inherited from Yugoslavia is that individuals can "buy" pension rights with respect to up to five years of higher education or military service, which then is counted as work. This is relatively cheap for the individual. Employers can buy pension rights for their employees, but this is more expensive: they must pay the whole cost of the additional pensions, unless they receive a subsidy from the NEO[52]. For some groups – *e.g.* the military, police and miners – the numbers of years of service are always multiplied by certain coefficients; in this case, the statutory retirement ages are also reduced in a corresponding manner. (They also pay higher annual contributions to the pension system.)

Detailed provisions

After a minimum 15 years of work, the standard retirement age is 65 for men and 60 for women. But most people work for at least 20 years, which from 1997 permits retirement at age 58 for women and 63 for men (following a gradual increase of these age limits since 1992, from 55 and 60, respectively). These are the "general" retirement ages.

Pensions are calculated as follows, always based on the average wage in a person's ten best-earning years, recalculated in after-tax terms to the level of the last income year. Once calculated, the pension is indexed according to the after-tax wage developments for working people. Women receive 40 per cent of their wage if they have 15 years of service, plus 3 per cent for each additional year. Men receive 35 per cent of their wage if they have 15 years of service, plus 2 per cent for the first ten additional years, thereafter 3 per cent per year. The ceiling is 85 per cent, thus corresponding to 30 years of service for women and 35 for men.

However, women having worked 35 years and men having worked 40 years can retire already at the age of 52 and 57, respectively – still with the maximum 85 per cent pension. These lowered age limits will be increased to 53 and 58 at the beginning of 1998[53]. They are, in effect, the normal retirement ages for persons having worked without interruption from age 17 (in 1998: 18), and also for many of those who can "buy" pension rights or whose years of service are increased by special rules.

The term "early retirement", as used in Slovenia (and in Table 4.3), does not cover the above provisions; it refers to a possibility for some groups to retire at age

53 (women) and 58 (men) after a work history up to five years too short – *i.e.*, after 30 and 35 years of work, respectively. Such "early retirement" is allowed if the worker is dismissed, following redundancy or bankruptcy, or has been registered as unemployed for 12 of the last 24 months. In this case, the pension is reduced by 1 per cent for each missing year of work, in addition to the automatic 2 or 3 per cent reduction. However, this additional cut of 1 per cent applies only until the retired worker reaches the age of 58 for women and 63 for men. As a result, the pension reduction is much smaller than it would have been if calculated by actuarial methods.

Insured persons who become disabled can obtain a pension at any age, if they lose their entire working capacity, otherwise often from age 45 for women and 50 for men. Apart from work-related disability and youths who become disabled before the age of 21, the applicant must have worked for a certain number of years, usually one-fourth to one-third of the time between age 20 and the day when the disability began. Disability pensions are reduced on the same basis as for early retirement, except in the case of work-related disability.

A ceiling applies to all pensions, at $(0.85 \times 310 =)$ 263.5 per cent of the average wage in the year in question. There is also a floor, at $(0.35 \times 64 =)$ 22.4 per cent of the average wage for women and $(0.40 \times 64 =)$ 25.6 per cent for men, or somewhat more for disability pensions, with a possibility for means-tested supplements.

In practice, relatively few retire before reaching their maximum entitlements. On average, persons retiring with old-age or early retirement pensions in 1995 were allowed to count 34 years of work, while those obtaining disability retirement had on average 26 years of service. As a result, in October 1996, the average amount of old-age and early pensions was about 63 000 Tolars after tax, *i.e.* three-fourths of the average wage, while the average disability pension was nearly 50 000 Tolars after tax[54].

Labour market implications

The net result of these provisions is that labour supply is low in all age groups from 50 and upwards. In part, this can be interpreted as a response to insufficient demand for certain groups of labour: roughly one-half of all retirements are justified by job displacements, long-term unemployment or disability. Nevertheless, the difference between the effective retirement ages in such cases and those obtained by other groups is often small. Most women and men seem to retire at ages near the median retirement ages of 53 and 57.5 years in any case, suggesting that the system's capacity to respond to different labour market signals cannot be very great.

Disability pensions currently account for about one-fourth of all pensioners in stock terms and one-third in annual inflow terms (not counting survivor pensions). As it appears, the rules about disability pensions can be attractive mainly for tenured workers who are only a few years younger than the usual retirement ages, while they are unattractive or inapplicable to most persons who are much younger or have relatively short work experience.

Apart from disability pensions, only 2 per cent of the women who retired in 1995 were younger than 50, while only 10 per cent of the men were younger than 55. The average numbers of working years counted were 35 for the women and nearly 40 for the men, indicating that many must have "bought" additional years or used the special calculation methods for certain jobs (most of which are dominated by men).

The median old-age retirement age for men has increased by over a year since 1992, but not so much for women. For women with disability pensions, the median age has even continued to fall. Overall, however, the trend appears to be increasing, as indicated by a rise in the employment/population ratio for the age group 50 to 64, from 34.5 per cent in 1994 to 36 per cent in 1996 (Table 1.3).

The new statutory retirement ages for women and men with over 20 years of service – 58 for women and 63 for men – are higher than similar limits in countries like the Czech Republic and Hungary, but there are plans for further increases in these countries as well. Some additional steps in the same direction appear justified in Slovenia, perhaps especially with regard to the reduced pension ages for persons with many years of service. Such a change could be combined with a stronger element of upward and downward variation in the pension amounts, following actuarial principles, for persons who opt for non-standard retirement ages.

CONCLUSIONS

Slovenia's transition has been relatively successful. After a temporary economic contraction in 1990 to 1992, its real GDP has returned to approximately the level it had reached before the transition. Employment remains lower, however, following many job losses in industry. The reduction especially concerned the age groups below 25 and over 50, whose employment/population ratios have become remarkably low by international standards. For the prime-age group of 25 to 49, by contrast, the employment/population ratio is still one of the highest in the world. Job creation has occurred predominantly in the service sector, largely through the growth of small firms, self-employment and temporary jobs. As a result, unemployment has stabilised near a moderate 7.5 per cent during the last two years.

The country remains highly industrialised, and has turned itself increasingly towards trade with Western Europe and the rest of the world, following the collapse of markets in the former Yugoslavia and other transition countries. In the current situation, with over half of its small economy depending on exports, Slovenia has little choice but to continue a policy of integration with the outside world. Employees have occasionally raised opposition to investment by foreigners, and there have been calls for protectionism and discriminatory public procurement – for example, in the 1996 Social Agreement between the government, employers and trade unions – but, on the whole, such defensive measures do not appear as the dominant policy approach. In general, the principles of international competition and free market access have gained broad acceptance, although the precise nature of the country's future participation in the European market integration are still somewhat uncertain.

In industry, there are many structural problems that urgently need to be dealt with, as reflected in a large number of unprofitable firms. Their ownership is frequently concentrated in the hands of employees, due to the way privatisation was achieved; surveys suggest that while these "insider" owners often take a long-term interest in their firms, they tend to have modest profit expectations and favour a cautious pace of restructuring. Another large group of shareholders are Investment Funds, often controlled by banks, whose capacity to play an active role in supervising and promoting the restructuring may be too limited. Against this background, a growing stock-market activity and more foreign direct investments could be useful in putting additional pressure on companies to become efficient.

A perhaps too cautious pace of restructuring has also been encouraged by the government's labour market policies, including some subsidies for preservation of jobs, and especially an employment protection legislation that can make redundancies quite expensive to employers. Firms that dismiss workers must pay wages for a six-month redundancy period, plus severance compensation. Furthermore, the law exhorts them to initiate individual adjustment measures, such as training, for the workers they intend to dismiss. To the extent that employers finance such measures, they may reduce the corresponding expenditure of the National Employment Office. In general, however, it is doubtful if the managers of enterprises in need of restructuring are better placed than the NEO to administer these measures. Worse, expectations that they will carry such social responsibilities may unduly distract their attention from their principal task, which is to make their businesses profitable and viable in the long term.

The NEO provides job brokerage, unemployment benefits and several programmes in support of employment and training. It also delivers vocational guidance and scholarships to students and issues work permits to foreigners. The office organisation has been extended in the 1990s, and now employs about 800 staff members, but less than half of them are in the local offices that handle the contacts with individual job-seekers and employers. For the future, it would seem important to simplify various administrative tasks and to move, as far as possible, the special functions concerning students to schools or other bodies, so that the NEO can concentrate on its core services to unemployed people. To facilitate its planning and management, it may also be justified to revise the budgeting procedures, with a view especially to the need for a more timely adoption of annual budgets than was achieved in the past few years.

The NEO's job-brokering relies to a great extent on self-service facilities, including a comprehensive listing of vacancies, published not only in and outside the offices but also in newspapers and through electronic media (Teletext and Internet). Employers must notify all job openings to the NEO, an obligation which is strictly enforced, contrary to the situation in some OECD countries with similar rules. Job notices are usually listed for a fixed application period, regardless of how quickly they are filled. As a result, many of the presumed "vacancies" concern jobs for which the employers already have candidates. It would appear justified to make the vacancy listing voluntary to employers, and to offer these a more diversified range of service options. The information value of the vacancy listing would be greater if it were limited to the cases where applicants are welcome. Special efforts could also be warranted, in co-operation between the NEO and employers, to enhance the quality of information provided about the notified jobs.

The job-seeker register, too, covers too many cases in which the need for NEO intervention is questionable. Many persons registered as "unemployed" actually have jobs, while others are not in the labour force, judging from labour force surveys – which, thus, suggest a much lower unemployment figure than the register does. On the other hand, there are probably many persons on the register who would need more job-search assistance than they currently receive. A problem, therefore, is that while the staff resources do not suffice to call all registered persons in for counselling with sufficient regularity, the very scarcity of these contacts can make it difficult to identify the individuals who might need them. In some regions, the offices have begun to organise compulsory monthly interviews for some groups of clients, especially unemployment benefit recipients; but in other cases, these contacts can be much less frequent. Another practice of increasing importance, following a model also used in OECD countries, is to organise focused interviews with every new client in order to determine the service needs and to assign a counsellor as a personal contact. In addition, the NEO has recently made special efforts to identify and remove irrelevant cases from its registers. Taken together, these activities may have contributed to some reduction in the number of unemployment benefit recipients, but there has been little change in the total number of the registered unemployed.

The unemployment benefit rules are more generous than in many other transition countries, and in certain respects they are comparable with some of the more generous systems in Western Europe. Thus, the insurance replaces 70 per cent of the lost income during the first three months of unemployment, then 60 per cent for up to 21 months, followed by a six-month period with a modest means-tested assistance. The total benefit duration can therefore be up to two and a half years, depending on the length of previous work experience.

However, less than one-third of the registered unemployed receive such benefits. First-job seekers and persons with under nine months of work experience are not compensated. The same is true of most of the long-term unemployed, once they have exhausted their entitlements, although those who are pensionable within three years can continue to collect benefits. Workers who leave their jobs without the employers' consent are always excluded, even if they remain unemployed for a long time. This last-mentioned rule may be too strict: it could discourage the unemployed and those working in unprofitable firms from trying new jobs that they are not sure if they want.

Expenditure on unemployment benefits have fallen since 1993, when their maximum duration was shortened; instead, more and more registered unemployed persons receive social assistance. The Centres for Social Work, which pay social assistance, require their able-bodied clients to register as unemployed at the NEO as well, but the NEO does not generally treat them with the same degree of priority as the recipients of unemployment benefits. Against this background, it could be justified to revise the two benefit systems and their administrative procedures, which in some respects can be regarded as a whole, with a view to the need for better co-ordination between the NEO and the Centres for Social Work. In principle, a similar amount of job-search assistance and availability controls would be pertinent with respect to all recipients of public income transfers for whom the main problem consists of unemployment.

The risk of unemployment is greatest for workers with few qualifications. In the younger age groups, about one-fourth of the labour force have no educational qualifications at secondary level. Many of them appear likely to remain in a vulnerable position for a long time, unless they can be helped to obtain marketable skills. In higher age groups, workers with little education have a strong tendency to leave the labour force, notably by taking retirement.

However, the NEO's measures for upskilling of unemployed adults are modest by international standards. Apart from some small schemes which mainly concern young adults, they consist essentially of a subsidy programme for on-the-job training. Slovenia's other resources for adult education are also relatively small, although currently being promoted by special policy efforts. Until now, the bulk of adult education has occurred in institutions for post-secondary education, to which many of the unemployed may find it difficult to gain access. A greater effort of job-related training for low-skilled workers could be justified.

The pension system will be difficult to finance in the long run, unless the average effective retirement age can be substantially increased. Some policy changes in this direction have been made, but the labour force participation rate remains markedly low in the age groups above 50. With the present rules, the financial incentives for individuals to work after reaching the lowest acceptable retirement age can be small, or even non-existent. In general, a more widespread use of actuarial principles for calculating pension amounts would seem justified, because this would permit a substantial enhancement of the work incentives, while still giving individuals an amount of free choice.

In sum, the economic transition has caused less social hardship in Slovenia than in most comparable countries. Several features of the social security system, including the fact that it has not faced insurmountable financing problems during the transition period, have evidently been important in explaining this favourable outcome. Moreover, many of the country's workers and employers have shown an impressive capacity to adjust to new conditions. In this context, however, the present report has noted a number of institutional shortcomings which seem to require continued policy action. By and large, the substance of these policy issues are henceforth quite similar to those which need to be addressed in other advanced economies. In Slovenia as elsewhere, a principal challenge is to facilitate, at acceptable social cost, a more or less constantly high pace of adjustment in enterprises in response to changes in the international market environment.

NOTES

1. One United States dollar was worth about 120 Tolars in 1995 and somewhat more in 1996. Compared with an average of OECD currencies, the exchange-rate value of the Tolar in 1995 was almost 90 per cent of its PPP value, while the corresponding proportion for most transition currencies was much lower (OECD, 1996b). Slovenia's GDP as measured by current exchange rates was therefore more than twice as high as in the Czech Republic.

2. Fischer et al. (1996) estimate that the real GDP decline from 1989 until the respective trough years was 16.8 per cent in Slovenia, 17.8 per cent in Poland, 18.3 per cent in Hungary and 21.4 per cent in the Czech Republic.

3. Information about companies is collected annually by the Gospodarski vestnik in collaboration with the Agency for Payments Transactions. See Slovenian Business Report (1996).

4. According to definitions inherited from the former Yugoslavia, employers are grouped in two main sectors, here and in the following referred to as the "commercial" and "non-commercial" sectors. The latter sector includes public authorities and some private service providers, especially in the areas of health care and education. (Sometimes, English-language literature uses different translations, e.g. the "economic" and "non-economic" sectors.)

5. LFS data for 1996 cited in this report are provisional. The surveys have been conducted in May every year since 1993, using household samples covering about 1.3 per cent of the population, with response rates in the range of 80 to 90 per cent. Smaller surveys were implemented from 1989 to 1992 by the Institute for Social Sciences, but they were regarded as a developmental project and the data were not intended for public use. The National Employment Office (NEO) managed the 1993 and 1994 surveys; this role has since been assumed by the National Statistical Office (NSO).

6. In the classification of educational attainment used by the LFS, as cited here and in the following, the category "less than two years of secondary education" includes some courses lasting up to two years.

7. The Adult Education Centre, established in 1991, conducts research and development in the area of adult education.

8. The NSO conducts monthly employer surveys (until 1992, RAD-1, thereafter ZAP-M), which currently cover establishments with three or more employees, and quarterly sur-

veys of smaller firms and the self-employed. Both probably tend to underestimate job creation in small- and medium-sized firms.

9. Matched individual records from the LFS in subsequent years, covering 1993 to 1996, were subject to special analysis for this study. The results may be biased by the fact that the interviews only concerned the situation in May.

10. The employment chances were estimated on the basis of Vodopivec (1996a, Table 5).

11. Annual LFS surveys may be distorted by seasonal factors, which are difficult to assess. In the past three years, the registered unemployment rates for May were less than half a percentage point below the respective annual averages, but seasonal variations may be greater in labour market sectors not covered by official registers.

12. The LFS regards as unemployed those who are jobless and ready to take jobs within two weeks, on condition that they have taken steps to seek work during the last four weeks.

13. Replies to LFS questions concerning registration at the NEO were analysed for the purpose of this study. The resulting LFS-based estimate of registered unemployment for May 1996 was 110 000, thus understating the actual 118 000. Here and in Tables 1.9 and 1.10, the relevant LFS figures have been adjusted on the assumption that the discrepancy was evenly distributed between different sub-groups among the registered unemployed.

14. This calculation was based on the (hypothetical) assumption that, in any year, approximately 27 000 young persons enter the labour market once.

15. Bartlett et al. (1996). See also Vodopivec (1996a), who estimates that the "socially-owned" sector, including public administration, accounted for almost 85 per cent of the employment in all industries in 1988.

16. At the exchange rate of the end of 1992, the vouchers were worth about US$ 1 000 to 4 000. See Albergo (1996, pp. 185-202).

17. The approved means of asset transfer in the context of privatisations include:
    – mandatory share transfer to state-controlled funds: 10 per cent to the Compensation Fund, 10 per cent to the Pension Fund, and 20 per cent to the Development Fund (for later sale to Special Investment Funds);
    – internal distribution (up to 20 per cent of shares can be traded to employees, former employees and their relatives in exchange for vouchers);
    – internal sale (a further 40 per cent of shares can be purchased by employees at a 50 per cent discount);
    – public sale of remaining shares through offerings, tenders or auctions;
    – liquidation of the company and sale of its assets;
    – sale of new shares to raise private equity;
    – transfer of remaining shares to the Development Fund.

18. The description of the previous wage-setting system draws largely on Vodopivec (1996a).

19. The term "wage" is used here in place of the former Yugoslav term "personal income". In theory, however – at least with regard to "socially owned" firms – an employee's "per-

sonal income" was considered to represent a share of the value added, including returns to capital as well as labour.

20. The importance of such procedures may not be very great if the formal conditions for their use are strict. In Germany, for example – where the conditions are similar to those now discussed in Slovenia – such "declarations of general validity" concern only a small percentage of the labour force.

21. The 1992 Law on Rates of Pay in Public Institutions, State bodies and Local Community Bodies, with amendments.

22. These figures, from the *Statistical Yearbook* (1996), cover all enterprises and public-sector employers with three or more employees.

23. The OECD-CCET labour market database.

24. After-tax wages were positively influenced by a cut in employees' social security contributions in 1992.

25. In October 1996, the average wage was 135 595 Tolars. After deduction of income tax and the 22.1 per cent social security contribution paid by employees, the take-home pay was 85 732 Tolars. Employers paid a 15.9 per cent contribution to the social security.

26. Law on Employment and Unemployment Insurance, Article 9.

27. About 28 000 employees, or 4 per cent of the dependent workforce, are classified as disabled.

28. Surveys by Chamber of Commerce, cited by Bival and Wörgötter (1995, p. 62).

29. During the 1980s, practically no federal government funds were allocated to social or labour market policies, apart from a small Federal Fund for Development of Less Developed Regions, to which Slovenia contributed along with other "rich" republics. The federal government tried to step up its own role after adoption of the new labour law in 1989. In 1990, it paid part of the cost of the new measures for redundant workers in enterprises, and in the budget for 1991 it envisaged – for the first time – a federal subsidy towards the unemployment insurance. At the same time, however, a centralising policy trend had begun to gain momentum within Slovenia (as in other republics), where the role of the numerous "self-managed" administrative bodies was increasingly questioned along with other specific features of the Yugoslav system.

30. Law on Employment and Unemployment Insurance, Article 9.

31. The LFS asks respondents who became employed in the previous year how they found their jobs, but the absolute number of respondents who mention private agencies has been too low in the survey samples to permit a reliable calculation of the percentage.

32. Such estimates were made in various OECD reviews of the public employment service, taking account for each country of the principal type of PES office dealing with individuals. Substantially larger average office sizes are found in a few countries, especially Germany (OECD, 1996a).

33. An official study in Switzerland, made in preparation for reforming the public employment service, recommended a target of 100 unemployed persons per placement officer, citing similar recommendations by other bodies which ranged from 80 to 150 (Arthur Andersen AG, 1994, p. 72). About 85 per cent of the unemployed in Switzerland at that time received unemployment benefits. OECD (1995a) found that the average job-broker in the Czech employment service had 100 unemployed clients, of whom about one-half received benefits.

34. The term "unemployment insurance benefit" is avoided here, because it has a different meaning in Slovenia compared with most countries. Elsewhere, it is often reserved for the more favourable types of benefit, and not considered to cover unemployment assistance (as it does in Slovenia). "Unemployment benefits", as used here, covers both types of benefit.

35. Elsewhere, as in Austria, Germany and Sweden, the benefit cut-offs for voluntary job quits usually last four to twelve weeks (OECD, 1996a).

36. In the United Kingdom, "new client" interviews commonly aim to develop a "back-to-work plan", which the benefit claimant must sign. The corresponding practice in Austria leads to individual "service plans", which however are not signed by the client. Elsewhere, as in Denmark, such procedures may apply mainly to the long-term unemployed (OECD, 1993, 1996a, 1996e).

37. In a few other countries, such as the Czech Republic and Switzerland, the unemployed must provide written proof from employers about their job search. This idea will now be tried in the Kranj region in Slovenia, in spite of some resistance from employers.

38. During 1996, such tests of availability for the purpose of the benefit administration appear to have been undertaken regularly in Maribor, but not in Kranj (where, however, they were used occasionally in connection with issuing work permits to foreigners – another NEO function).

39. The reported number of sanctions in 1995 was 328, to which should perhaps be added an unknown number of cases when the NEO may have simply removed unco-operative individuals from the register. In other countries, too, formalized sanction procedures often seem to be avoided, although they are sometimes more frequent than in Slovenia. Contrary to the Slovenian practice, the resulting benefit cut-offs in many countries have relatively short duration. See, for example, OECD (1996a).

40. Law on Employment and Unemployment Insurance, Article 32.

41. Some OECD countries have sought to reduce the weight of control functions by separating the Public Employment Service from the unemployment benefit administration. Separate office networks for the latter function are found, for example, in Belgium, France and the United States. In general, however, OECD reviews have suggested that the job-brokering will in any case be influenced by its role as a necessary complement to the benefit administration.

42. The Law on Employment and Unemployment Insurance, Article 9, obliges employers to notify the NEO within eight days after a recruitment need is identified. The deadline for

job applications must be at least eight days thereafter. Also, Article 10 requires employers to inform the NEO annually by 15 January about recruitment needs in the coming year.

43. Unofficial estimate submitted by the NEO.

44. According to OECD (1996e, Table 4), the vacancy flow into the public employment service in 1994 corresponded to 15 per cent of the dependent labour force in Norway and to between 10 and 12 per cent in Germany, Japan, Sweden and the United Kingdom. Similar estimates elsewhere were lower.

45. The estimate of the numbers not formally registered was derived from the 1996 LFS. The relevant legal provisions are in Article 16 of the Law on Employment and Unemployment Insurance.

46. Evaluation results in Canada and the United Kingdom were quoted in OECD (1993, p. 56). Recent developments, especially in the United States, have aimed to develop more formalized and detailed procedures for "profiling" of new job-seekers, aimed at facilitating early identification of persons at risk of long-term unemployment.

47. Another relatively large subsidy programme was introduced in 1995 by the Ministry of Economic Activities, with about 5 billion Tolars paid to firms which were net exporters and exposed to unfavourable exchange rates, covering their social security contributions for up to six months. A condition was that the firms respected certain wage restraints included in the Social Agreement. This programme was not continued in 1996.

48. In forestry, these provisions concern redundancies considered to result from certain changes in property law, which transferred decision-making powers from the timber industry to forest owners.

49. The number of recipients of supplementary benefits continued to increase in the first five months of 1996, reaching almost 30 000.

50. The remaining 1 600 social assistance recipients in 1995 obtained a slightly more favourable type of benefit, amounting to 60 per cent of the guaranteed income. They were essentially disabled or elderly persons.

51. The cited overall average of 52 years represents a weighted mean of the medians, as estimated separately for each gender and for the two main types of pension.

52. In the early 1990s, a high proportion of those obtaining early retirement could benefit from NEO grants, which covered part of the employers' expenses for "buying" additional years for redundant workers.

53. Thus, the gradual increase of these lower age limits will be completed one year later than the corresponding increase of the standard limits.

54. The difference between pensions and average wages is greater before tax.

BIBLIOGRAPHY

ALBERGO, G. (1996), "Outlook for Slovenia", *PlanEcon Review and Outlook for Eastern Europe,* July.

ARTHUR ANDERSEN AG (1994), *Réforme du service public de l'emploi en Suisse,* OFIAMT, Zurich.

BARTLETT, W., PRASNIKAR, J. and VALENCIC, D. (1996), "Employment growth in small firms in Slovenia", Faculty of Economics of the University of Ljubljana, mimeo.

BIVAL, G. and WÖRGÖTTER, A. (1995), *The Republic of Slovenia,* Institute for Advanced Studies, Vienna.

BRADA, J. (1996), "Privatisation is transition – or is it?", *Journal of Economic Perspectives,* Vol. 10, No. 2, Spring.

FISCHER, S., SAHAY, R. and VÉGH, C.A. (1996), "Stabilisation and growth in transition economies: the early experience", *Journal of Economic Perspectives,* Vol. 10, No. 2, Spring.

IMAD (INSTITUTE OF MACROECONOMIC ANALYSIS AND DEVELOPMENT) (1995), *Slovenia: Analysis of Economic Trends in 1995 and Projections for 1996,* Ljubljana, Autumn.

IMAD (1996a), *Slovenia: Analysis of Economic Trends in 1996,* Ljubljana, Spring.

IMAD (1996b), *Slovenian Economic Mirror: August-September 1996,* Ljubljana.

JAKLIN, J. (1995), "First assessment of privatisation results in Slovenia 1995" (preliminary report), Country Privatisation Report, Central and Eastern European Privatisation Network, mimeo.

MOLFSA (MINISTRY OF LABOUR, FAMILY AND SOCIAL AFFAIRS) (1996), "Information on persons entitled to financial supplement under the law on social assistance in the period from 1.7/31.12.1995", Ljubljana, mimeo.

NATIONAL STATISTICAL OFFICE (1994, 1995 and 1996), *Statistical Yearbook,* Ljubljana.

NEO (NATIONAL EMPLOYMENT OFFICE) (1996), *Annual Report 1995,* Ljubljana.

OECD (1993), *The Public Employment Service in Japan, Norway, Spain and the United Kingdom,* Paris.

OECD (1994), *The OECD Jobs Study, Evidence and Explanations,* Part II, Paris.

OECD (1995a), *Review of the Labour Market in the Czech Republic,* Paris.

OECD (1995b), *The Public Employment Service: Denmark, Finland, Italy,* Paris.

OECD (1996a), *The Public Employment Service: Austria, Germany and Sweden,* Paris.

OECD (1996*b*), *Short-term Economic Indicators: Transition Economies,* No. 3, Paris.

OECD (1996*c*), *A Review of the Swiss Labour Market, Paris.*

OECD (1996*d*), *Employment Outlook,* Paris.

OECD (1996*e*), *Enhancing the Effectiveness of Active Labour Market Policies,* Paris.

ORAZEM, P., VODOPIVEC, M. and WU, R. (1995), "Worker displacement during the transition: experience from Slovenia", Ljubljana, mimeo.

PODKAMINER, L. (1995), *Transition Countries: Economic Developments in Early 1995 and Outlook for 1995 and 1996,* Vienna Institute for Comparative Economic Studies, Research Reports No. 219 and 220, Vienna, July.

SLOVENIAN BUSINESS REPORT (1996), Ljubljana, Fall.

VODOPIVEC, M. (1996*a*), "The Slovenian labour market in transition: evidence from micro-data", *Lessons from Labour Market Policies in the Transition Countries,* OECD, Paris.

VODOPIVEC, M. (1996*b*), *Transition from Cash Benefits to Work: The Case of Slovenia,* OECD workshop on the Transition from Unemployment to Social Assistance.

MAIN SALES OUTLETS OF OECD PUBLICATIONS
PRINCIPAUX POINTS DE VENTE DES PUBLICATIONS DE L'OCDE

AUSTRALIA – AUSTRALIE
D.A. Information Services
648 Whitehorse Road, P.O.B 163
Mitcham, Victoria 3132   Tel. (03) 9210.7777
Fax: (03) 9210.7788

AUSTRIA – AUTRICHE
Gerold & Co.
Graben 31
Wien I   Tel. (0222) 533.50.14
Fax: (0222) 512.47.31.29

BELGIUM – BELGIQUE
Jean De Lannoy
Avenue du Roi, Koningslaan 202
B-1060 Bruxelles Tel. (02) 538.51.69/538.08.41
Fax: (02) 538.08.41

CANADA
Renouf Publishing Company Ltd.
5369 Canotek Road
Unit 1
Ottawa, Ont. K1J 9J3   Tel. (613) 745.2665
Fax: (613) 745.7660

Stores:
71 1/2 Sparks Street
Ottawa, Ont. K1P 5R1   Tel. (613) 238.8985
Fax: (613) 238.6041

12 Adelaide Street West
Toronto, QN M5H 1L6   Tel. (416) 363.3171
Fax: (416) 363.5963

Les Éditions La Liberté Inc.
3020 Chemin Sainte-Foy
Sainte-Foy, PQ G1X 3V6 Tel. (418) 658.3763
Fax: (418) 658.3763

Federal Publications Inc.
165 University Avenue, Suite 701
Toronto, ON M5H 3B8   Tel. (416) 860.1611
Fax: (416) 860.1608

Les Publications Fédérales
1185 Université
Montréal, QC H3B 3A7   Tel. (514) 954.1633
Fax: (514) 954.1635

CHINA – CHINE
Book Dept., China National Publications
Import and Export Corporation (CNPIEC)
16 Gongti E. Road, Chaoyang District
Beijing 100020 Tel. (10) 6506-6688 Ext. 8402
(10) 6506-3101

CHINESE TAIPEI – TAIPEI CHINOIS
Good Faith Worldwide Int'l. Co. Ltd.
9th Floor, No. 118, Sec. 2
Chung Hsiao E. Road
Taipei   Tel. (02) 391.7396/391.7397
Fax: (02) 394.9176

**CZECH REPUBLIC –
RÉPUBLIQUE TCHÈQUE**
National Information Centre
NIS – prodejna
Konviktská 5
Praha 1 – 113 57   Tel. (02) 24.23.09.07
Fax: (02) 24.22.94.33
E-mail: nkposp@dec.niz.cz
Internet: http://www.nis.cz

DENMARK – DANEMARK
Munksgaard Book and Subscription Service
35, Nørre Søgade, P.O. Box 2148
DK-1016 København K   Tel. (33) 12.85.70
Fax: (33) 12.93.87

J. H. Schultz Information A/S,
Herstedvang 12,
DK – 2620 Albertslung   Tel. 43 63 23 00
Fax: 43 63 19 69
Internet: s-info@inet.uni-c.dk

EGYPT – ÉGYPTE
The Middle East Observer
41 Sherif Street
Cairo   Tel. (2) 392.6919
Fax: (2) 360.6804

FINLAND – FINLANDE
Akateeminen Kirjakauppa
Keskuskatu 1, P.O. Box 128
00100 Helsinki

Subscription Services/Agence d'abonnements :
P.O. Box 23
00100 Helsinki   Tel. (358) 9.121.4403
Fax: (358) 9.121.4450

*FRANCE
OECD/OCDE
Mail Orders/Commandes par correspondance :
2, rue André-Pascal
75775 Paris Cedex 16 Tel. 33 (0)1.45.24.82.00
Fax: 33 (0)1.49.10.42.76
Telex: 640048 OCDE
Internet: Compte.PUBSINQ@oecd.org

Orders via Minitel, France only/
Commandes par Minitel, France
exclusivement : 36 15 OCDE

OECD Bookshop/Librairie de l'OCDE :
33, rue Octave-Feuillet
75016 Paris   Tel. 33 (0)1.45.24.81.81
33 (0)1.45.24.81.67

Dawson
B.P. 40
91121 Palaiseau Cedex   Tel. 01.89.10.47.00
Fax: 01.64.54.83.26

Documentation Française
29, quai Voltaire
75007 Paris   Tel. 01.40.15.70.00

Economica
49, rue Héricart
75015 Paris   Tel. 01.45.78.12.92
Fax: 01.45.75.05.67

Gibert Jeune (Droit-Économie)
6, place Saint-Michel
75006 Paris   Tel. 01.43.25.91.19

Librairie du Commerce International
10, avenue d'Iéna
75016 Paris   Tel. 01.40.73.34.60

Librairie Dunod
Université Paris-Dauphine
Place du Maréchal-de-Lattre-de-Tassigny
75016 Paris   Tel. 01.44.05.40.13

Librairie Lavoisier
11, rue Lavoisier
75008 Paris   Tel. 01.42.65.39.95

Librairie des Sciences Politiques
30, rue Saint-Guillaume
75007 Paris   Tel. 01.45.48.36.02

P.U.F.
49, boulevard Saint-Michel
75005 Paris   Tel. 01.43.25.83.40

Librairie de l'Université
12a, rue Nazareth
13100 Aix-en-Provence   Tel. 04.42.26.18.08

Documentation Française
165, rue Garibaldi
69003 Lyon   Tel. 04.78.63.32.23

Librairie Decitre
29, place Bellecour
69002 Lyon   Tel. 04.72.40.54.54

Librairie Sauramps
Le Triangle
34967 Montpellier Cedex 2 Tel. 04.67.58.85.15
Fax: 04.67.58.27.36

A la Sorbonne Actual
23, rue de l'Hôtel-des-Postes
06000 Nice   Tel. 04.93.13.77.75
Fax: 04.93.80.75.69

GERMANY – ALLEMAGNE
OECD Bonn Centre
August-Bebel-Allee 6
D-53175 Bonn   Tel. (0228) 959.120
Fax: (0228) 959.12.17

GREECE – GRÈCE
Librairie Kauffmann
Stadiou 28
10564 Athens   Tel. (01) 32.55.321
Fax: (01) 32.30.320

HONG-KONG
Swindon Book Co. Ltd.
Astoria Bldg. 3F
34 Ashley Road, Tsimshatsui
Kowloon, Hong Kong   Tel. 2376.2062
Fax: 2376.0685

HUNGARY – HONGRIE
Euro Info Service
Margitsziget, Európa Ház
1138 Budapest   Tel. (1) 111.60.61
Fax: (1) 302.50.35
E-mail: euroinfo@mail.matav.hu
Internet: http://www.euroinfo.hu//index.html

ICELAND – ISLANDE
Mál og Menning
Laugavegi 18, Pósthólf 392
121 Reykjavik   Tel. (1) 552.4240
Fax: (1) 562.3523

INDIA – INDE
Oxford Book and Stationery Co.
Scindia House
New Delhi 110001   Tel. (11) 331.5896/5308
Fax: (11) 332.2639
E-mail: oxford.publ@axcess.net.in

17 Park Street
Calcutta 700016   Tel. 240832

INDONESIA – INDONÉSIE
Pdii-Lipi
P.O. Box 4298
Jakarta 12042   Tel. (21) 573.34.67
Fax: (21) 573.34.67

IRELAND – IRLANDE
Government Supplies Agency
Publications Section
4/5 Harcourt Road
Dublin 2   Tel. 661.31.11
Fax: 475.27.60

ISRAEL – ISRAËL
Praedicta
5 Shatner Street
P.O. Box 34030
Jerusalem 91430   Tel. (2) 652.84.90/1/2
Fax: (2) 652.84.93

R.O.Y. International
P.O. Box 13056
Tel Aviv 61130   Tel. (3) 546 1423
Fax: (3) 546 1442
E-mail: royil@netvision.net.il

Palestinian Authority/Middle East:
INDEX Information Services
P.O.B. 19502
Jerusalem   Tel. (2) 627.16.34
Fax: (2) 627.12.19

ITALY – ITALIE
Libreria Commissionaria Sansoni
Via Duca di Calabria, 1/1
50125 Firenze   Tel. (055) 64.54.15
Fax: (055) 64.12.57
E-mail: licosa@ftbcc.it

Via Bartolini 29
20155 Milano   Tel. (02) 36.50.83

Editrice e Libreria Herder
Piazza Montecitorio 120
00186 Roma   Tel. 679.46.28
Fax: 678.47.51

Libreria Hoepli
Via Hoepli 5
20121 Milano   Tel. (02) 86.54.46
                    Fax: (02) 805.28.86

Libreria Scientifica
Dott. Lucio de Biasio 'Aeiou'
Via Coronelli, 6
20146 Milano   Tel. (02) 48.95.45.52
                    Fax: (02) 48.95.45.48

JAPAN – JAPON
OECD Tokyo Centre
Landic Akasaka Building
2-3-4 Akasaka, Minato-ku
Tokyo 107   Tel. (81.3) 3586.2016
                    Fax: (81.3) 3584.7929

KOREA – CORÉE
Kyobo Book Centre Co. Ltd.
P.O. Box 1658, Kwang Hwa Moon
Seoul   Tel. 730.78.91
                    Fax: 735.00.30

MALAYSIA – MALAISIE
University of Malaya Bookshop
University of Malaya
P.O. Box 1127, Jalan Pantai Baru
59700 Kuala Lumpur
Malaysia   Tel. 756.5000/756.5425
                    Fax: 756.3246

MEXICO – MEXIQUE
OECD Mexico Centre
Edificio INFOTEC
Av. San Fernando no. 37
Col. Toriello Guerra
Tlalpan C.P. 14050
Mexico D.F.   Tel. (525) 528.10.38
                    Fax: (525) 606.13.07
E-mail: ocde@rtn.net.mx

NETHERLANDS – PAYS-BAS
SDU Uitgeverij Plantijnstraat
Externe Fondsen
Postbus 20014
2500 EA's-Gravenhage Tel. (070) 37.89.880
Voor bestellingen: Fax: (070) 34.75.778

Subscription Agency/Agence d'abonnements :
SWETS & ZEITLINGER BV
Heereweg 347B
P.O. Box 830
2160 SZ Lisse   Tel. 252.435.111
                    Fax: 252.415.888

**NEW ZEALAND –
NOUVELLE-ZÉLANDE**
GPLegislation Services
P.O. Box 12418
Thorndon, Wellington Tel. (04) 496.5655
                      Fax: (04) 496.5698

NORWAY – NORVÈGE
NIC INFO A/S
Ostensjoveien 18
P.O. Box 6512 Etterstad
0606 Oslo   Tel. (22) 97.45.00
                    Fax: (22) 97.45.45

PAKISTAN
Mirza Book Agency
65 Shahrah Quaid-E-Azam
Lahore 54000   Tel. (42) 735.36.01
                    Fax: (42) 576.37.14

PHILIPPINE – PHILIPPINES
International Booksource Center Inc.
Rm 179/920 Cityland 10 Condo Tower 2
HV dela Costa Ext cor Valero St.
Makati Metro Manila Tel. (632) 817 9676
                     Fax: (632) 817 1741

POLAND – POLOGNE
Ars Polona
00-950 Warszawa
Krakowskie Prezdmiescie 7 Tel. (22) 264760
                           Fax: (22) 265334

PORTUGAL
Livraria Portugal
Rua do Carmo 70-74
Apart. 2681
1200 Lisboa   Tel. (01) 347.49.82/5
                    Fax: (01) 347.02.64

SINGAPORE – SINGAPOUR
Ashgate Publishing
Asia Pacific Pte. Ltd
Golden Wheel Building, 04-03
41, Kallang Pudding Road
Singapore 349316   Tel. 741.5166
                    Fax: 742.9356

SPAIN – ESPAGNE
Mundi-Prensa Libros S.A.
Castelló 37, Apartado 1223
Madrid 28001   Tel. (91) 431.33.99
                    Fax: (91) 575.39.98
E-mail: mundiprensa@tsai.es
Internet: http://www.mundiprensa.es

Mundi-Prensa Barcelona
Consell de Cent No. 391
08009 – Barcelona   Tel. (93) 488.34.92
                    Fax: (93) 487.76.59

Libreria de la Generalitat
Palau Moja
Rambla dels Estudis, 118
08002 – Barcelona
     (Suscripciones) Tel. (93) 318.80.12
     (Publicaciones) Tel. (93) 302.67.23
                     Fax: (93) 412.18.54

SRI LANKA
Centre for Policy Research
c/o Colombo Agencies Ltd.
No. 300-304, Galle Road
Colombo 3   Tel. (1) 574240, 573551-2
                    Fax: (1) 575394, 510711

SWEDEN – SUÈDE
CE Fritzes AB
S–106 47 Stockholm Tel. (08) 690.90.90
                    Fax: (08) 20.50.21

For electronic publications only/
Publications électroniques seulement
STATISTICS SWEDEN
Informationsservice
S-115 81 Stockholm Tel. 8 783 5066
                    Fax: 8 783 4045

Subscription Agency/Agence d'abonnements :
Wennergren-Williams Info AB
P.O. Box 1305
171 25 Solna   Tel. (08) 705.97.50
                    Fax: (08) 27.00.71

Liber distribution
Internatinal organizations
Fagerstagatan 21
S-163 52 Spanga

SWITZERLAND – SUISSE
Maditec S.A. (Books and Periodicals/Livres
et périodiques)
Chemin des Palettes 4
Case postale 266
1020 Renens VD 1   Tel. (021) 635.08.65
                    Fax: (021) 635.07.80

Librairie Payot S.A.
4, place Pépinet
CP 3212
1002 Lausanne   Tel. (021) 320.25.11
                    Fax: (021) 320.25.14

Librairie Unilivres
6, rue de Candolle
1205 Genève   Tel. (022) 320.26.23
                    Fax: (022) 329.73.18

Subscription Agency/Agence d'abonnements :
Dynapresse Marketing S.A.
38, avenue Vibert
1227 Carouge   Tel. (022) 308.08.70
                    Fax: (022) 308.07.99

See also – Voir aussi :
OECD Bonn Centre
August-Bebel-Allee 6
D-53175 Bonn (Germany) Tel. (0228) 959.120
                       Fax: (0228) 959.12.17

THAILAND – THAÏLANDE
Suksit Siam Co. Ltd.
113, 115 Fuang Nakhon Rd.
Opp. Wat Rajbopith
Bangkok 10200   Tel. (662) 225.9531/2
                    Fax: (662) 222.5188

**TRINIDAD & TOBAGO, CARIBBEAN
TRINITÉ-ET-TOBAGO, CARAÏBES**
Systematics Studies Limited
9 Watts Street
Curepe
Trinidad & Tobago, W.I. Tel. (1809) 645.3475
                         Fax: (1809) 662.5654
E-mail: tobe@trinidad.net

TUNISIA – TUNISIE
Grande Librairie Spécialisée
Fendri Ali
Avenue Haffouz Imm El-Intilaka
Bloc B 1 Sfax 3000 Tel. (216-4) 296 855
                    Fax: (216-4) 298.270

TURKEY – TURQUIE
Kültür Yayinlari Is-Türk Ltd.
Atatürk Bulvari No. 191/Kat 13
06684 Kavaklidere/Ankara
                    Tel. (312) 428.11.40 Ext. 2458
                    Fax : (312) 417.24.90

Dolmabahce Cad. No. 29
Besiktas/Istanbul   Tel. (212) 260 7188

UNITED KINGDOM – ROYAUME-UNI
The Stationery Office Ltd.
Postal orders only:
P.O. Box 276, London SW8 5DT
Gen. enquiries   Tel. (171) 873 0011
                    Fax: (171) 873 8463

The Stationery Office Ltd.
Postal orders only:
49 High Holborn, London WC1V 6HB
Branches at: Belfast, Birmingham, Bristol,
Edinburgh, Manchester

UNITED STATES – ÉTATS-UNIS
OECD Washington Center
2001 L Street N.W., Suite 650
Washington, D.C. 20036-4922
                    Tel. (202) 785.6323
                    Fax: (202) 785.0350
Internet: washcont@oecd.org

Subscriptions to OECD periodicals may also
be placed through main subscription agencies.

Les abonnements aux publications périodiques
de l'OCDE peuvent être souscrits auprès des
principales agences d'abonnement.

Orders and inquiries from countries where Dis-
tributors have not yet been appointed should be
sent to: OECD Publications, 2, rue André-Pascal, 75775 Paris Cedex 16, France.

Les commandes provenant de pays où l'OCDE
n'a pas encore désigné de distributeur peuvent
être adressées aux Éditions de l'OCDE, 2, rue
André-Pascal, 75775 Paris Cedex 16, France.

                                    12-1996

OECD PUBLICATIONS, 2, rue André-Pascal, 75775 PARIS CEDEX 16
PRINTED IN FRANCE
(14 97 09 1 P) ISBN 92-64-15606-2 – No. 49665 1997